PENN
PENN

7lb plus bass, Cardigan Bay (1992)

7lb bass, Cardigan bay (1990)

6lb plus shore bass, Cardigan Bay (1987)

Blue shark, Off Union Hall (1989)

Mike releasing a blue shark, Union Hall (1989)

Mike with his first ever common skate – estimated 170lb, Clew Bay (1994)

Mike and 35lb shore caught tope, Cardigan Bay (1995)

Mike and 55lbs shore caught tope estimated by length and girth, Cardigan Bay (2001)

Mike and tope over 80lbs about to be released, Cardigan Bay (1997)

Mike and a 9lb 2oz barbel, River Wyc, Hereford (1999)

Mike with a mixed bag of barbel, chub and dace, River Wye, Hereford (1999)

Mike with a 40lb amberjack, Florida Keys (November 1999)

Mike with his first ever sailfish, Florida Keys (November 1999)

A shore caught 15lb nurse shark, Florida Keys (February 2002)

Mike's 250lb bull shark, Florida Keys (November 1999)

Loading the Land Rovers for the trip up the Gambia river (2000)

Mike's accommodation near the mouth of the Gambia River (2000)

Gambian River catfish (2000)

Mike initially fishing for the tilapia (2000)

Mike's tilapia (2000)

The saw jaw from a 20-feet plus sawfish, Gambia River (2000)

Mike with a 40lb captain fish, Mouth of the Gambia River (2000)

Mike with two captain fish to 40lbs, Mouth of the Gambia River (2000)

A sizeable yellowfin tuna coming aboard, Punta Colorado, Mexico (April 2001)

Mike playing the big yellowfin tuna on the PENN Slammer Stik Rod, ABU 7000C reel and 18lb line, Punta Colorado, Mexico (April 2001)

Mike holding an estimated 70lb yellowfin tuna, Punta Colorado, Mexico (April 2001)

Mike with a 45lb bull dorado, Punta Colorado, Mexico (May 2001)

Punta Colorado Beach in front of the hotel where Mike lost the big Jack Crevalle (June 2002)

Mike with his 35lb roosterfish, Punta Colorado, Mexico (June 2002)

Mike with a jack crevalle caught on light spinning tackle, Punta Colorado, Mexico (June 2002)

Mike with a 4lb surf perch caught fly fishing in the surf, Punta Colorado, Mexico (June 2002)

Mike's blue marlin leaping, Punta Colorado, Mexico (June 2002)

Abu Garcia
SINCE 1897

FOX

PENN

Abu Garcia
Abu Garcia

PENN
Shakespeare

PENN

PENN

PENN
PENN

PENN

37lbs Icelandic boat caught cod

A rare long rough dab caught from Isafjordur Iceland

A fly caught cod of 6lb 5oz from the shore off Grimsey Island, Iceland

Fly caught coalfish in Iceland

Near 5lb haddock caught off the shore from Isafjordur Iceland

Rare Icelandic starry ray

Mike with a shore caught halibut of 15lbs 10oz caught near Hasvig - Norway

Mike with his personal best Norwegian cod of 38lbs caught off Loppa

A fly caught coalfish of 8lbs caught off Senja Norway

Fly caught boat haddock weighing 4lbs 11oz off Senja Norway

MIKE THRUSSELL

Addicted to Angling

A lifetime's obsession with
fish and fishing

Peridot
Press

First published in 2015 by Peridot Press Ltd
12 Deben Mill Business Centre, Melton, Woodbridge, Suffolk IP12 1BL

ISBN: 978-1-909717-47-3

Set and designed by Theoria Design
www.theoriadesign.com

Contents

"This book is exactly what I hoped it would be; full of fishing anecdotes as well as Mike's angling story. What's more it's written in such a way that I can actually hear Mike telling the tales as I read the words. Unless you are an angler it is difficult sometimes to appreciate what we have and how lucky we are to have it. Mike's seminal work will without doubt be able to bring the definition of why we fish to everyone, whether they have ever held a fishing rod or not."

Keith Arthur, Sky Sports' *Tight Lines*

"Mike Thrussell's Addicted to Angling gets to the heart of the sport – a personal contest between man and fish, a pursuit with remarkable highs and its fair share of lows.
As a leading angling journalist, Mike has woven an engaging tale of his pursuit of a multitude of species at home and abroad. But it's more than a personal journey, being packed with all those must-have nuggets of advice that have made Mike such a highly regarded angling writer."

Cliff Brown, Editor, *Sea Angler* Magazine

"Mike Thrussell is a rare bird: an angler's angler and a writer's writer, and in Addicted To Angling he has shown us the best of both. Addicted To Angling is a book of stories, of rigs, and of fish catching tips, delivered in Mike's deceptively easy style. In more ways than one, this is, the angling book of a lifetime."

Paul Dennis, Editor, *Total Sea Fishing* Magazine

"I've known and fished with Mike for nearly twenty years. This book reflects some of the great stories and achievements from that time, and beyond. A great read from one of the UK's most experienced and respected sea anglers."

Dave Barham, Editor, *Boat Fishing Monthly Magazine*

Introduction

Without someone still unknown to me, I may never have written this book. A suggestion, based on the books I wrote over 25-years ago, by that anonymous person, led to an email asking if I may be interested in writing another book. Since those original books, all those years ago, I've spent my working life writing articles and features about fishing, mainly sea fishing, for monthly magazines. I've also been heavily involved in tackle product development for major tackle companies, as well as other forms of work allied to sea angling. With these day to day commitments, finding the time to write a lengthy work again, was difficult, and for the most part impossible. The idea always seemingly pushed to the back burner. It was something I had considered many times, in fact hoped, and even wanted to do, but as so often in life, something unexpected needs to occur that opens the door and encourages you to take the decisive step and finally commit to a new opportunity.

The word 'unexpected' is apt, for it is what this book is about. It's about some of my experiences, the amazing people, and more so the adventures I've been lucky enough to live, on what has proved a winding road that's taken me round many hidden bends. The words and stories in this book will not just be drawn from memories. Since my early teens I've religiously kept a written diary of every fishing trip I've ever made, always written within a few hours of my return. The diary serves many purposes, recording vital information that, over time, comes together to improve your chances of catching fish. More importantly, once written, the pages never lie, unlike an ageing mind that can sometimes reflect a difference of opinion. As I write this book, story by story, chapter by chapter, I will turn the relevant pages of my diaries to recount, and re-live, those adventures exactly as they unfolded.

I don't want this book to be about all the successes that have occurred either. I also want to tell you about some of the mishaps, the mistakes I've made, and the big fish lost, though to be fair Lady Luck has more often been with me more than against me. Only a handful of fish have been lost that I really look back on with real regret, and you'll learn of these in the pages to come. Sometimes we learn more from a fish lost, than one caught.

This book, as the title says, is initially about a boy, then a man, with an insatiable addiction to angling. Though inevitably the book will be read by the reader through my eyes and words, my hope is that my passion, for what in my opinion is the king of all sports, is to give you the desire to go out and fish and experience some of the pleasures sea angling, and angling in general, has given me. Ultimately, my aim is to pass on that addiction!

Mike Thrussell
June, 2015

Foreword By Nick Fisher

When I was planning to buy a new fishing boat and didn't know which brand to get, I called Mike Thrussell. When I was starting a fishing series on BBC 5 Live and needed a sea fishing consultant, I called Mike Thrussell. When I was researching a shark fishing segment for my angling TV series *Screaming Reels* and needed to know where and when we could film a shark sequence, I called Mike Thrussell.

I have to confess I have picked Mike's brains about all things sea-angling, from holiday destinations to beach casting rigs. When I wrote *The River Cottage Book of Sea Fishing,* there was only one set of eyes I'd trust to check it for howling mistakes and schoolboy errors...

Mike's sea fishing knowledge is not only encyclopaedic; it's beautifully instinctive. Mike knows things about fish and fishing, locations and techniques, but he also *feels* things too. His knowledge is not just cerebral, it's also instinctual in a way that can't be taught or even learned. Salt water flows through Mike Thrussell's veins. There are, I believe significant traces of sea fish apparent in his DNA.

I trust Mike's opinion and views because I know he doesn't formulate or proffer them lightly; his opinions are born of much thought, sound research and years of first-hand, coal-face experience. Mike has served his time. Done his ten thousand hours and more, to earn the mantle of 'expert'. And yet, it's not a label he would use easily of himself. For all his knowledge he remains unerringly modest.

It's what makes him such a fertile font of wisdom. Some men make you feel small when you ask them for advice. They like to spout and proclaim in a manner that can make you sorry you ever asked. Not Mike. His experience and advice are always offered with a self-effacing wit.

What this book proves beyond all shadow of doubt is that Mike's knowledge is his own. Not borrowed or bastardised, not book-learned, or plagiarised, but divined from devoting an enormous part of his life, to not just fishing – all over the world – but recording every single day spent rod-in-hand, with forensic accuracy.

I've been lucky enough to have fished in a few of the locations Mike mentions (Iceland, Florida, Norway, Gambia) but I only have a tiny collection of blurred photos and even more blurred memories. Because to do what Mike does – record, photograph, make detailed diary entries – is very hard work. It doesn't happen by accident. His discipline as a photo-journalist and writer is testament to his dedication. Me, I fish, I eat and I forget. Not Mike. He creates a record from which others can learn.

That's why I could never write a book as true and exact as this one, and can only marvel and admire the breadth and depth of its meaty detail.

What Mike's book also does is give me inspiration of places I long to fish. Thanks to Mike's meticulous work I can identify places for my bucket-list of angling destinations.

So, if you want ideas of where in the world to wet a line, they're in here. If you want to know how to cobble together a rig to catch a marlin with a spinning rod – it's here. But what this book can't teach you, *or* me, is how to develop the instinct, the sixth sense, the nose for fish that Mike Thrussell posesses. That is not something that can be explained.

'Addiction' is a strong and often negative term. When we're addicted, we're out of control of something that ultimately does us harm. Eats away at us. Lessens us. Although Mike has described his love of fishing as an addiction, it is far from being a negative attribute, more of a creative one. His addiction is our gain. His obsession conveyed so enthusiastically is not a cautionary tale from which we recoil, but a beautifully crafted catalyst to make us want to get up, get out and go forth to investigate new horizons and new species.

The fact that Mike releases nearly every fish he catches means that his book is not a document of greed and victory: he has no desire to kill - he is not some great white hunter of great whites - but a man who loves his fishing most when the fish survives.

Mike's book is not about the struggle of man over Nature – instead it's about moments of connection between man and fish, in a variety of wonderful wild locations.

Between these pages lies a gripping confession, not so much of an addiction but of a passion that Mike has enthusiastically pursued his entire life and which has shaped him into the man he is today.

The man I call whenever I need to know *anything* about the sea and the things that swim.

Nick Fisher 2015

Chapter 1
The Early Days

There is a memorable quote, attributed to Francis Xavier, a 16th century Basque Roman Catholic Missionary, "Show me the boy at seven, and I'll show you the man". It seems the actual wording of this phrase has been lost over the years, but no matter. It eludes that the character, interests, and future path of the man already lay within the boy by the age of seven. In my case, this seems to have been true.

There were no anglers in my immediate family to fire my passion for fishing as a child. I remember my father, a skilled engineer, professionally building race and rally cars at the time, these cars taking part in the RAC Rally, Monte Carlo and Tulip rallies, and winning awards, was given by a customer a fishing book and, bizarrely, an Australian Alvey side cast reel. The customer said, "Give these to your son. He might be interested". That book was *Mr Crabtree Goes Fishing*, initially written by Bernard Venables as a comic strip in the *Mirror* newspaper in the 1940s, then as a book, which is now a classic work. I was not yet school age, but remember being fascinated by the illustrations, repeatedly flipping through the pages. This book, as it did for so many, lit a spark that smouldered in my head waiting to fully ignite.

We lived near the steel city of Sheffield on the Derbyshire border. Both my parents worked hard, but at every opportunity we visited the coast, often camping near Barmouth in North Wales. I remember, after weeks of pestering the old man, walking in with him, to what was then a corner shop called All Sports And Hobbies near the railway station in Barmouth, to buy my first rod and reel. That first rod was some seven feet long and a grey, solid glass spinning type rod. The owner, John (unfortunately I can't remember his surname), was a good retailer and he selected an appropriate reel that matched the rod for size and balance, chose some 10lb monofilament line, picked out a few lead weights, swivels, hooks and a few beads, put the terminal tackle in a brown paper bag, wished us well, and I walked out of the door pleased as punch. I spent a fair bit of pocket money with John over the next few years.

Duly kitted out and bursting with enthusiasm, my Dad picked some mussel for bait off the rocks in front of the caravan and I made my first ever tentative cast in to the mysterious waters of the Mawddach Estuary. The cast could not have gone far, yet, after what probably seemed like an age to me, the rod tip trembled then pulled round, and I reeled in a flounder. This on my very first ever cast and at the tender age of about four. My dad, as a non-fisher person, was as surprised as I was. That fish, probably no more than a pound in weight, looked huge to me at the time. Although there was no way to know it, this flounder was to be the key that unleashed an unquenchable thirst to fish. I remember catching little from there on for quite a few holidays, if truth be known, yet never did I get bored or despondent. I'm told I would sit on the rocks, casting, re-baiting, watching the rod tip, eyes never flinching, enduring wind, rain and cold, such was my obsession and preoccupation. Most kids quickly lose patience under similar circumstances, their minds quick to wander and investigate something more animate. Not me! I was transfixed for the duration, intent solely on catching fish, whatever that may require, and whatever physical or mental pain I had to endure to do it.

The only opportunity I had to actually go fishing during those initial years were on vacations taken during the national holidays. For me the gap between New Year and Easter, with no chance of fishing, was unbearable. The time span from Easter to Whitsuntide less so, usually being only a few weeks. The two weeks holiday we took in July or August was the crock of gold at the end of the rainbow. Except for brief excursions with the family I would fish every day in to dark, and was often up at the crack of dawn, quietly getting dressed, easing the caravan door open, then gently shutting it, fearful of waking the 'oldies'. Retrieving the already made-up rod from under the caravan and making off to the estuary channel and a land of wonder and excitement.

Once at school, and with improving reading ability, I started to read the fishing magazines. Reading is not the right word, I devoured them, cover to cover, word for word. I remember spending pocket money on *Creel*, also *Angling Times* and *Anglers Mail*, these being the first. I loved reading the catch reports and marvelled at some of the monsters caught. Then, a little later, I discovered *Angling Magazine*. Its pages shed light on a world where anglers didn't just go fishing, they learnt about the habits and habitat of the fish they sought, their feeding preferences, seasonal migrations, then designed tackle specifically to target that individual species. It was a mine of how-to-catch information which I willingly soaked up and stored. Books came next, and my collection, either bought by myself, or gained as Christmas and birthday presents, grew at a pace.

When I wasn't fishing, I was sorting and tidying tackle, attempted my first tentative rig making, and commandeered the old man's shed to make various items of tackle, some successful, some not so. I also started to buy bare blanks and build my own rods. Skills that at the time were hard for a young fella to learn, but again, without knowing it, once mastered, I was building for the future.

I caught my first whiting, dabs, eels, rockling and dogfish. My Dad and I booked one of the Barmouth Ferry boats after ferry hours and the skipper took us fishing just outside the mouth of the estuary...and I loved it. I also ventured off to sample freshwater fishing. Worming for trout, but also perch fishing in Gwernan Lake below Cader Idris, then Llyn Cynwch near the market town of Dolgellau. One day, again on the Mawddach Estuary, I struck in to a fish that fought way better than any of the others I'd caught previously. The rod tip whipped round, the rod nearly sliding off my tackle bag it was leant against. I grabbed the rod, the fish already hooked, and I took a deep breath as the fish pulled hard for its freedom, the reel clutch actually giving line and me in a self-admitted state of panic, not quite sure what to do. The fish was fighting close in to the rock I was standing on, its grey blue flanks and silver white belly flashing as it twisted and turned. I'd never seen a bass prior to this, but instantly recognised what I had on the end of my line. I remember feeling my way to the edge of the water, reaching down to grab the line above the fish, and lifting it, all in one movement, up on to a rock ledge and safety. It probably weighed a couple of pounds or so, but at the time it was the biggest fish I'd caught. I felt like a Stone Age hunter walking back to the cave, my fish proudly dangling from my left hand, but already thinking about the next one. This first bass was a catalyst that pushed me on to more targeted fishing.

In time we left the Derbyshire moors and moved, lock, stock and barrel, to Machynlleth, not far from the coast in mid Wales, and soon moved again to a little village right on the coast near Tywyn. Now the sea was accessible daily and I got to fish much more regularly. In to my teens, and still a devotee of the angling magazines, I got to favour the work of the late John Darling. John was a bass angler, a skilled writer and photographer, but also an observer. His writing on bass excited me. It was fluent, detailed, articulate, but, as I found out later, deadly accurate in its fact. His early writing saw him speak in detail about bass from the rough ground on the Sussex coast where he lived. Some of what he described I recognised on my own coast. I spent all available time looking at and analysing the beaches, studying their changing character. I started to catch bass too, decent bass of four and five pounds sometimes, yet never the big fish that John seemed to catch. It was at this time that I started to learn the pendulum cast. At the time a new concept casting style designed to bring in to play the more powerful muscles of the body to increase casting range. With no one to ask or show me how to do it, I remember endlessly casting, and snapping numerous leads off in a field, after reading an article by Dennis Darkin in, yes, you guessed it, *Angling Magazine*. It was a slow, painful, and all too frequently line-costly learning curve, but eventually I got there. Again it was a skill that would be put to good use later on.

Though still fishing, on passing my driving test, I also got in to rallying and to some surprise found out I was pretty quick. Somehow I also had the ability to keep the car on the road and not bend it too often. I loved rallying. It was exciting coupled with an element of danger. It required some skill at the wheel to be consistently fast, anticipation, smoothness, and was incredible fun. But it was very expensive and, though working now, my wallet did not have the depth to fund it long term. Sadly it had to go.

Life was about to throw me her first real shock. Work was not easy to find during the early 1970s in North Wales. I worked for myself mostly, but early on also had a series of jobs without finding anything that really suited me. At a loss as to what to do with my future, in the mid 1970s, out of the blue, I had the chance to go to Australia to work. It was an opportunity I grabbed with both hands, even though, at the time still shy of 20 years-of-age, leaving the UK for somewhere new and unknown frightened me to the core.

I was based in Rockingham initially, to the south of the West Australian capital, Perth. I was about to get married too, so work became a real priority. The Australians, God bless them, who were incredibly kind and generous in their friendship to me, love their weekends and free time, and while working alongside a couple of Aussies they asked me what I did for fun. I mentioned that I fished and as we all know, fishing is a friend-maker the world over. I was instantly invited out fishing with them. My first forays took me after bluefish and many varieties of saltwater bream on the sandy beaches at Safety Bay, also for flathead in the estuary at Mandurah, then snapper from the rock marks and jetties. As time went on my horizons expanded and I targeted bronze whaler sharks off the shore, hitting sharks that would have been well over 100lbs and losing much bigger ones, some never even seen after a long, dogged fight, before the line gave, or they cut through the wire traces. This flirtation with big fish was another seed that would lay dormant for some years within me, then flower and grow to magic beanstalk proportions.

Though Australia was great for me, eventually I had to return to the UK. I was sad to leave such a wonderfully free and open country. I chose to come back to my fishing roots in North Wales. It was 1980. Having mostly been self-employed so far, I chose the same route again, and once a work life was established my thoughts quickly turned to the beaches I'd fished before I went abroad. Even in Australia my thoughts would sometimes wander to the bass beaches of my youth. I would mindlessly drift away, feel the sharp salt wind on my face, hear the surf crash and rumble out in the dark, feel the surge of the flood tide against my legs, sense the cold, slim butt of the rod cradled in my hands, then feel the smash-and-grab bite of a hungry bass. My mind was made up. I was going to concentrate on bass...

Chapter 2
Bass

To specifically target bass, I needed a strategy. What I'd learned in the past was that the simple act of fishing was not enough. It made sense to pick out three or four venues, then fish them hard through every conceivable weather and tide variance throughout the year. I would make detailed observations and notes, these to include wind direction and speed, tide height and size, the time and state of the tide, water clarity, cloud cover or lack of, sea state rough or calm, the surf pattern, and anything else that came to mind at the time as being important. I did not put a defined season in place for bass either. My mind was open. I would fish throughout the year and see what occurred, then formulate the best time by results alone.

I initially picked out four venues. One a sandy surf beach, two rough ground beaches, and a small estuary. Three different ground features, but a mix that would deduce where my best opportunities lay. I spent a lot of time the first winter just walking the beaches over low water during the bigger tides when the ground was fully visible, studying the ground feature as I had in the past. It was clear that the ground, and some individual feature, would change with every storm. This especially applied to the sandy surf beaches. The gutters and gullies were constantly shifting. A southwest storm would flatten out the gullies. A northwest storm would move them in or out, or change their direction along the beach. It struck me that if I was struggling to comprehend what was happening on a daily basis, so too might the fish. I never believed for one moment that fish are simple minded. They are intelligent to a degree that helps them survive in a harsh environment where 'kill or be killed' is the simple rule. No mean feat! I could see, in certain conditions, that bass certainly would feed on the surf beach. More than likely after storms when food had been washed from the sand. Walking the beach, what concerned me was the lack of obvious food during average surf and weather conditions. Being a west-facing storm beach there were a few worm casts at the end of the beach where some shelter was found from the prevailing wind next to cliffs, the odd sand clam or Tellin could be picked up. At low water on a big spring tide the jets of water made by razorfish burrowing as they felt the pressure of your weight confirmed they were present, but it was pretty much all I saw. To my eyes, a sandy beach was where bass were mainly in transit, picking off any food items they came across, but purposefully heading to pastures new where the feeding was richer.

Walking the rough ground beaches proved my thoughts. My wanderings over the shallow, rocky reef and boulder-strewn ground revealed numbers of small fish such as shannies, small wrasse and gobies, sometimes mottled brown and gold butterfish in the shallow pools left by the outgoing tide. The rocks housed colonies of mussel, and their shells, as well as razorfish shells, littered the beach, especially after a good storm when they had been torn free and smashed against the rocks. But one food source really stood out. Crab...and lots of them. These were mainly common shore crab, but you would also find velvet swimming crab, edible crab, and various other small swimming crab towards the low water mark. Just as I'd read and briefly experienced previously, my best chance was on the rough ground, with crab likely to be the most effective bait. Crab was also the most common food item for much of the year found in the stomach contents of caught bass. The evidence was all-conclusive!

The small narrow-channelled estuary I had in mind, I wanted to fish for a different reason. My thinking was that the bass ran the estuary pretty much every tide to feed on the weedy edges where crab were hiding, as well as other food items such as sandeel, small fish, shellfish, worm and anything else that was flushed out by the pushing tide. If I could find the perfect points and ambush the bass as they passed by, I was confident that my baits would be eaten by my intended quarry. What's more, the main channels being relatively narrow, the majority of bass would have to pass by me within casting range, dramatically increasing my chances.

Having established that shore crab were an important food item for bass, I bought scientific papers on the life cycle of the common crab, *Carcinus maenus*. I learnt that to grow, the crab has to dissolve its shell by extracting chemicals from the shell's composition until it becomes brittle. The crabs then take in seawater to swell the new soft body inside and gradually, literally like a big man struggling out of a tight overcoat, when the top back shell becomes brittle enough to crack away, they struggle out of the old shell and leave it behind. The crab, now having a totally soft shell, must hide somewhere safe, half buried in mud, under stones or weed, while the new soft shell re hardens. The process varies on weather and water temperature, but takes a few days in all, though it can take longer in cool weather. Though bass take hard-back crabs naturally, for many reasons they do not work as a bass bait. In contrast, a just-popping peeled peeler crab oozing scent, or a fresh juicy soft crab, will have a bass come homing in on it from 30 yards away.

Due to the time and information gathering I'd put in prior to fishing, when I did wet a line I did not have to wait too long to make some encouraging catches off the rough ground. My first few trips in the April and May of 1982 produced bass to 4lbs. I was averaging a fish of size, every two or three trips. Then in June I caught fish of 5lb 7ozs and 6lb 2ozs amongst numerous smaller ones. I was heading in the right direction. I always fished alone at this time, so had no one else to compare with, but over the next few seasons I learnt a lot from my careful and detailed diary.

The bass came on the rough round in small numbers about the middle of April. Their numbers built through May, with June giving a high likelihood of a number of fish. July through to mid August the bass would be offshore working the sandeel and mackerel shoals. However the occasional fish would turn up in bizarre circumstances on the rough ground, such as a hot, calm, bright sunny evening with no surf and a flat calm sea. By late August the fish would come back. Fat now, full bodied and healthy. They moved back on to the rough ground in September, and some would stay until mid November, before they move out on to the open beaches and leave the smaller sub-3lb bass to forage the stone. What I had come to realise was that the bass had set routes they travelled over the rough ground and boulders, and specific set times of tide they visited certain areas. Their predictability proved my gain, and I came to know exactly where and how to give myself the best chance of success.

AN EVENING TO REMEMBER

Glancing at the tide table, I saw low water was at 18.40. It was a good tide, a 28-footer based on Liverpool data, and rising towards bigger spring tides. The wind was a steady force 3 and forecast to go force 4 after low water. Looking out of the window the cloud was lowering, cloaking the mountain in a grey obscuring haze, a sign of rain to come. Being June the wind, though damp, was warm as I walked across the shingle, then down across the broken ground, a mix of some sand, but mostly rock, to the low water line. The tide was still just ebbing away, but I positioned myself at the head of a little gutter that ran slightly deeper than the surrounding ground in front of me. No point fishing yet. I had to wait until the tide actually turned.

I was fishing a light 2-4oz, 11ft rod matched to a well used ABU 6500 multiplier reel loaded with 20lb mono. The 20lb line was to combat the rocks and barnacles should it get abraded, either while fishing, or when fighting a fish. The rod I'd built myself. It was light to hold, had no reel seat to minimise weight, just reel clamps to retain the reel in place. The rig was a simple sliding paternoster designed so that the hook trace was attached directly to the main line to maximise bite detection through to the rod tip. At just nine inches long, the 20lb hook trace would register even the lightest of bites. The 1.5oz weight was attached via a length of 15lb mono to a swivel sliding freely on the main line that jammed up against the swivel tied to the hook trace. The lighter 15lb line would intentionally break before the main line if the lead weight got snagged. I found that the lighter lead weights had several advantages. They were less likely to snag in amongst the rocks, and would often bounce around as the surf tables washed over them giving the bait more natural presentation.

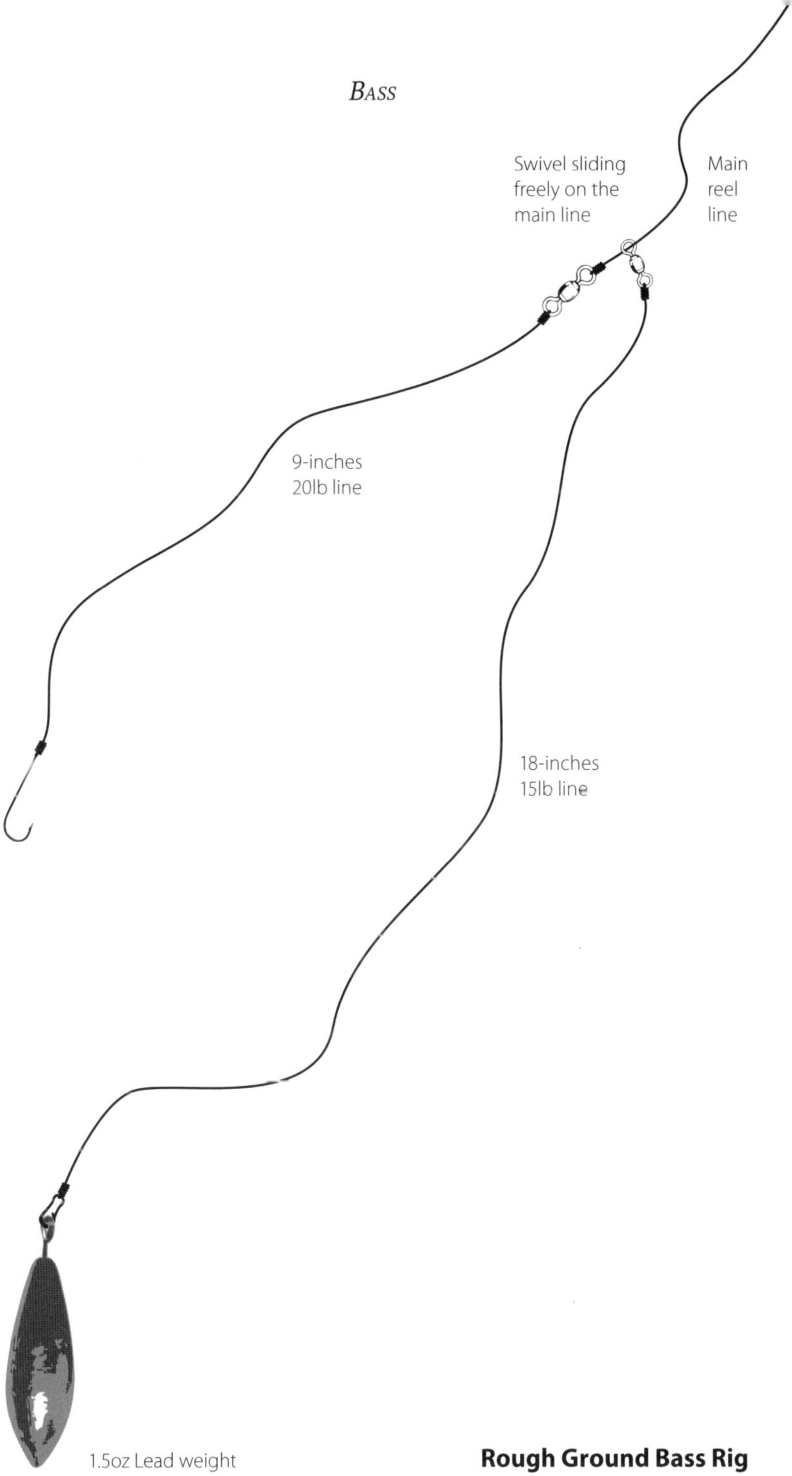

Rough Ground Bass Rig

Taking a fresh but dead peeler crab, I peeled off all the brittle shell. Cut the body lengthways in two, slid one half up over the hook on to the shank, and hid the hook point with three peeled crab legs leaving the ends of these hanging free to make it look as natural as possible. I watched the white turning surf tables. The tide was now just pushing making its first searching runs of the new flood. I lobbed the bait in to the little gully just 25 yards out. I held the rod low across my stomach, rod tip pointing downwards and away from me at a slight angle, the line just taut against the weight. This mark would give me a chance of just two casts before a shallow gully behind me started to flood and I would have to move.

I fished the first cast for 15 minutes, then re-baited. Crab can wash out quickly in the surf tables and a fresh bait full of juice doubles your chances. The second cast fell in exactly the same place, right in the middle of the little gully. Time always passes quickly when I'm fishing. My mind would concentrate so hard, time was of little consequence. The tide was rising quickly now, pushed in by the increasing wind. A light drizzle began to fall. A glance to both sides confirmed I was totally alone on the shore, just an occasional gull cried an equally lonely lament.

I sensed the bass before I actually felt it. Gut instinct, a sixth sense, call it what you will, but I was aware the bass was there. I felt the line tighten a fraction, then the rod tip slid forward. I responded with an uplift of the rod and felt the tip curl over to a real alive weight. The bass had nowhere to go, except to turn round and power down the gully for freedom. In doing so, it made the drag on the reel purr as it gave a little line, and I noticed little jets of water spit up off the line as it left the spool. When you hit a good fish, things seem to play out in slow motion, your senses heightened, your eyes taking more in than normal. It doubled back coming towards the shore, me frantically winding the reel handle to keep the line tight. I could see the fish, lunging, turning, trying to make short runs back out to sea. Its head came up and I knew it was beaten. It looked about 6lbs as I slid the fish in to my feet.

The gutter behind me was already awash with water. I travel light when bassing: just the rod and reel, a few spare rigs and leads in a coat pocket, and a bucket of crab, the bucket with a sealable lid in case the surf should ever wash it over, for as you see, you need to be mobile. I grabbed the bucket and waded thigh deep through the gutter. I'd got 10 minutes to quickly walk a couple of hundred yards up the length of the beach to reach another gutter, re-bait and cast. This mark could produce two or three bites in a 25 minute period before again I would have to move.

I baited with a big juicy soft crab this time, just lobbed out no more than 20 yards in to a deep bowl at the head of the gutter. I settled in, head down against the driving drizzle, rod low to the water and the line tight. The rod inert and lifeless in my hand bar for the slight pull on the line as the surf tables washed over it. Suddenly the tight line was gone, dropping back in a slack bow towards me. Lifting the rod and winding the reel to gain line at the same time, the rod again bent to a good fish. I had to hold this fish hard as if it got back in to the deeper gutter, there was a sharp rock shelf that would snip my line like scissors. It was stalemate for a minute or so, the bass battling it out in front of me, trying to turn for the open sea, me letting the rod dip as opposed to allowing line to peel off the drag so as not to over-pressure the line or the hook hold. The fish was smaller, maybe 4lbs. Baiting with another big soft crab, the bait went back out in to the bowl. Instantly the rod hammered over and another fish, bigger this one, steamed out back in to the gutter dragging line with it. Heavy pressure turned the fish before it reached the shelf. It wallowed, head went down, and it bored off again. This fish had weight and it was hard to control it. Dropping the rod to both sides to confuse the fish worked and it came back in to the deeper bowl in front of me. I allowed it to tire itself out then, lifting the rod, I slid my forefinger and thumb either side of the lower jaw to grip the fish and lifted it in. I figured a shade better than 7lbs, a short bodied, stocky fish, heavy behind the head. The last cast here produced nothing, and I had to cross open water to get to my last spot, some 300 yards away.

A big boulder the size of a car, stood like a lone sentinel amongst much smaller boulders. The sea had washed out the boulders around its base leaving finer shingle in its place. At low tide a pool of water was always present around the big boulder. It was a natural food trap. Anything pushed along by the tide would be deposited in the depression at the boulder's base. Bass will always work round the base of big boulders. The tide was already flooding the boulder and I just had time to bait up, this time with a half of a big peeler crab. Standing back from the boulder maybe 30 yards, I dropped the bait almost hard up against the rock. Using the light leads, if they moved, you needed to just retighten the line occasionally. If the lead weight skidded across the shingle, you struck, as it might be a fish. The tide was pushing hard now, sending searching waves forward, filling in all the holes, depressions and deeper areas. Two feet of water now washed the boulders base. The line went slack against the rod. I felt the weight drag across the shingle and the line tighten as I struck. Sometimes the fish would bore down and try and get behind the boulder. This one, against the grain, went away from the boulder in an uptide direction. It thumped the rod tip as it shook its head, screamed off taking line off the reel, turned, and went back out to sea. It swung downtide this time and I needed side pressure to turn it. It went back uptide and I saw its tail and

Mike playing a 5lb plus Bass (1987)

back briefly break surface. Again it turned towards me, head up on the surface, and I slid it in to my waiting hand. Another fish about 6lbs and as fat as butter. The last cast here produced another smaller fish about 4lbs.

I'd fished a little over two hours, caught five bass, two 4lbers, two 6lb fish, and one over 7lbs. What's more it was by design. Gone was the chuck and chance it approach of my youth. All those days of fishing hard, making mistakes, learning from them, making notes, learning the weather patterns, getting the tides right, and coming to know exactly where the fish would be at certain times all came together to produce quite a few nights and mornings like the one described. It had been a massive learning curve, gleaning information from others, but mainly by trial and error on my own part. I think back now and during this time I was probably more at one with the sea and saltwater environment than at any time since.

AN HOUR AT THE BAR, JUST TIME FOR A BASS

The rough ground fishing was only half the story. At the same time I was learning the ways of the estuary bass too. This was equally fascinating, and with some similarities to the rough ground fishing. What I came to realise was that, for the most part, April and May were not good months in the estuary. The smaller school bass would be there, sub-3lb fish mostly, but the bigger fish were mainly on the rough ground beaches elsewhere.

What brings the bigger bass in to the estuaries is the main explosion of peeler crab over the big tides that occur towards the end of May, and again in the middle and towards the end of June. Due to the warming sea temperatures, and to some extent air temperature, the crabs peel en masse. No bass will ignore this bountiful food supply. Towards the end of May bass stocks inside the estuaries suddenly take a huge turn for the better, and with them come the big fish. However my best fishing was always in the autumnal months of September and October. Although the crab peel is well past its best by then, small explosions still occur around the big tides, and the bass know it too.

I'd also come to understand that these smaller estuaries tend to have a bar of sand evident, this being the demarcation line between the open sea and the beginning of the main estuary channel. The bass group up on the outside of the bar, then run the main channel as soon as the flood tide turns. They use the tide to push as far up the estuary as they can, before using the outgoing ebb tide to bring them back out to sea, feeding as they go, but without expending much energy.

It was early October. I'd been watching the TV weather forecast closely. The wind had been light southerly for several days, but was due to swing southwest and pick up to near gale force. Low tide was 2.40 am. It was a 30.2-foot tide. Perfect for a big bass. I had my gear ready to go, and got a little broken sleep until 1.30am. I rose, gulped down some hot coffee, and was heading for the estuary before 2am. Walking the sand towards the bar of the channel, the tide was still ebbing. The wind had risen and was blowing maybe 30mph. It was a chill wind, not bitter, but damp, the type that makes your cheeks glow after time spent outdoors. I could hear the surf out in the distance, a dull rhythmic, almost tired rumble.

I checked back at the town lights and took a mental bearing where the higher sand was using the streetlight as a beacon. These outer bar areas are scattered with deeper channels, gutters and washed out holes. Making sure you know the way off is vital when wading back through a shallow flooding tide in the pitch black with just a headlight to guide you. I reached the main channel and decided to fish on a high bank of sand some 100 yards in from the bar. On this size of tide, it was as near as I could get. Glancing at my watch it was 2.25am.

I readied my gear, the same rod and reel I used on the rough ground. This time though, the lead weight would be 3ozs as I need to cast to range, a 70 yard cast usually necessary to reach the main run of fish. I prepared six halves of crab, the reason being the fish can come through fast over a short period of time, and time lost by peeling crabs after a fish has been caught means fewer casts made and less fish hooked.

Much like on the rough ground, I'd got to know the mannerisms and character changes of the estuary. I always fished at night in the dark. When doing so, your senses are heightened and you become aware of the unseen around you. It must be a faint link back to when we hunted for a living with spears, but it remains, buried deep in our being. I got so used to fishing the bars of the small estuaries that I could truly hear the tide turn. Many do not believe this, but some experience the same, and it is a fact. The ebb tide surf has a low, subdued rumble to it. When the tide turns it increases in activity, the surf becomes a louder, energetic crash, its mood almost like an excited child at Christmas. This increase in energy is perceptible to the ear if you experience it enough to learn it.

Standing alone in the dark, I heard the note of the surf tables change. I glanced at my watch: it was 02.37. The wind had turned the tide early. I made a long cast in to the main channel, felt the lead hit the seabed, tightened to it, and fell back in to my preferred rod-across-the-lower-chest stance to feel for bites. Almost instantly a bite came. The fish was hooked, but carried no weight. It was a school bass about 2lbs. The next cast produced another. This also told me that while the little fish ran, you are unlikely to hit a big one. The big ones like more water depth over the bar before they run, but also will not compete with the little fish, which get the bulk of the food first when in direct competition. If you watch and note, there is always a pause inbetween the school bass running through, and when a big fish hits. At least it is in my experience.

A third school bass took the crab bait and was released. I cast again, half expecting an instant rattle as another little bass made off with the bait. Nothing happened! Perhaps ten minutes went by. I was holding the rod, still concentrating, when the rod tip, without warning, crashed down as a massive weight engulfed the crab, turned back in to the tide flow, and swam away. I struck, but in truth the hook was already home and solid in the jaw of the bass. Its weight was obvious, the rod bent hard over and line grudgingly ticking off the reel as the drag surrendered. The bass, slow but powerful in its movement, heading down tide and out in to the deeper channel. Rod pressure made it turn and it now headed uptide for maybe 20 yards, then turned back downtide again. I started to gain line, slowly at first using small upward pumps of the rod and gaining just inches of line. The bass resisted, turned, and headed back out in to the deeper water. It shook its head, me conscious that the hook might simply fall out as it did so. I was gaining line now, but a shallow bank in front of me was an obstacle I had to steer the fish around. In my headlight I saw the fish wallowing on the surface. A giant tail beating side to side and churning the water white. I walked to my right a few feet and with a little side pressure steered the fish away from the bank in front. Its head was briefly out of the water and I could see it was big. It made two short bursts seawards, but that sapped its strength and it turned on its flank and I slid it on to the sand. Though I rarely take a fish now, any fish in fact, in those far off days things were different, and I kept the odd fish for the pot, as I did this one. It weighed 9lb 8ozs exactly. It was the last fish of the session, there would be no more as the fish had run through and were well gone.

NEVER TO BE FORGOTTEN

It didn't always go to plan mind. There was one night on the estuary that is etched in my mind forever. It was early October. Glancing at my watch as I topped the sand dunes it was just past 3am, 25 minutes before low water. The wind was in the west and nearly gale force. It was raining hard too, the driving rain that hammers on your coat and hood. The surf, over the bar, was big, heavy and crashing. I could see the white rollers turn over even in the near pitch black. Reaching the channel, the tide, a big spring tide over 32-feet, had not pushed back as far as I'd expected, held back by the strong wind.

I'd tackled up back at the car. I'd rigged with a newly released hook from a well known UK company. A fine wire type with a mini barb. I figured the lighter hook and small barb would get a better grip when striking in to fish at long range.

Just before low water I baited up with a big peeler crab, cut in half and bound lightly with bait elastic to release lots of scent. Casting out maybe 60 yards in to the edge of the deeper water, just above a series of small sand banks arranged like the fingers of man's hand with shallow water in between, I felt the lead touch down and grip. The first two casts produced nothing. The tide had turned now. I heard it turn as I so often did, but also could see the first push at the waters edge when I turned my headlight on. The third bait I cast a little further in to the deeper water beyond the channel edge.

Standing on the sand banks, there was a hint of cold in the wind. The cheeks on my face tingled with both the cold and the incessant rain. My hands, holding the rod across and slightly upwards off my chest were also numbing and cold due to the elements. My mind, educated to it over the previous years, was concentrating on the rod tip, the line and the bait, feeling for any perceptible change in pressure, but also for the heart-stopping savage lunge of a taking bass. That's exactly what I got. One second the rod was inert, lifeless and disinterested. The next the tip slammed over. I instantly struck sweeping the rod backwards and upwards. The rod took on a serious curve that I felt deep down in the butt section as the weight of the fish came to bear. The fish powered off downtide as it felt the hook. This was a big fish. I just knew straight away from the feel of it. It shook its head, tore off taking more line, then doubled back uptide and almost gave slack line, which I just managed to recover. A series of savage head shakes now, then serious weight thumping way out in the darkness.

I kept steady pressure on the fish, gradually working it, inch by inch, towards me. I felt hot, even sweaty now, and could feel my heart pounding like a drum. I felt the fish was close, then caught a glimpse of white water as it swirled on the surface. It was uptide of the little sand banks as I was leading it in towards me aiming to beach it on the sand at my feet. The fish though, turned its head for the sea, its huge tail making white water as it pumped itself back deeper and further away almost dragging line off the reel in slow motion. It turned its head downtide heading for the finger shaped sand banks. I applied side pressure, but the fish would not turn. Then I saw it in my headlight. It was semi beached at the end of a finger of sand, half in, half out of the water. I kept light pressure on the rod and started to wade towards it. The fish rolled and its great flank, just 15 yards or so away from me, came in to view. It was huge! It flopped on its side, tried to paddle its tail, and a sudden weight pulled the rod tip down as the fish rolled again...then the rod sprang back. Shock instantly hit me. That dull, hurtful, all-consuming pain that settles in the gut of your stomach. Realisation clicked in and I started to run towards the fish. The fish, sensing freedom, lazily from fatigue slowly swung its tail side to side, wriggled its body, and in just inches of water slid slowly out of sight. It was gone!

I remember standing there, a sick empty feeling still in the pit of my stomach, my mouth dry and my heart still pumping. I just kept staring at where the fish had been and was in total denial of what had just happened. Questions raced through my mind. "The hook must have pulled out, the hook trace broken, maybe a knot gave out?" "Why, why, why?" I retrieved the line and swung the trace in to me. Everything was there, intact. The hook must simply have pulled out! There was nothing for it, but to re-bait and cast again, though I felt defeated, angry and frankly just wanted to go home. The new bait ready, I picked up the hook. Only then did I notice it had broken right underneath the barb and as clean as if you had cut it with hacksaw. The hook point must have been in tough gristle inside the mouth of the bass and only just barb deep. With the weight of the mighty fish all on the point, the hook broke at the weakest point where the pressure was greatest, at the barb. I never used those hooks again.

You'll be asking by now, how big was the fish? I can only judge on what I saw on a dark windswept night, in heavy rain at 15 yards or so distance, and what I felt through a rod that had become part of my being through constant fishing. The depth of the flank is what stood out. My guess, and that's all it can ever be, was a fish in excess of 15lbs. It took me a week or more to get over the loss. In fact, even now, though I should know better, it hurts when I think of it. Why, and all too often, is it the fish of a lifetime that gets away because of an unusual occurrence?

FLY BY BASS

I was not one for competitive fishing, but did enter a week long species competition held on the island of Alderney in October of 1991. There were categories for individual fish, the idea being that the biggest weighed in of a species would win that category. The trip out to Alderney was a scheduled flight from Southampton. I was travelling with some friends mainly from the Wirral area, and we had a lot of tackle to take. It was also very windy. The pilot was a Biggles-like character, and clearly a seasoned flyer. As we were boarding he said that the plane was as heavy as allowed due to our tackle, some of which had to be flown out on later flights, that the wind was on the limit, and that we might have a difficult landing on Alderney. He was right!

As we approached Alderney the pilot took two passes over the island to gauge the wind and how it would affect his landing. One of these passes took us relatively low but right over Bray Beach. As I looked back at the beach from the port side window I saw a finger of rock jutting out roughly mid-way along the beach, and here, with the wind in the west quarter, there was a big swell running. I felt this would be a good place to target a bass when the competition time opened.

That night, Wirral angler Phil Simpson and I walked the beach towards the rock finger. The wind was strong from the west with a 30.1-feet tide. The sea was rough with a big surf and it was carrying weed. Phil went on the left of me, but I wanted to cast as close to the rocks as I could, and right where the surf was building as it ran in along the length of the rocky finger. I baited with ragworm and made several long casts out to the edge of the rocks. I had little tappy bites that resulted in small pouting.

As the tide increased in height, so to did the power of the surf. It was difficult fishing now. I made a cast very tight in to the rocks, but with the wind blowing hard the cast was not too long and probably only about 70 yards out just to where the big waves were building. I was stood, in the dark, water washing around my legs, holding the rod across me when I felt the familiar hammer blow on the rod tip as a bass took the bait. I instinctively hit it. I felt a solid weight, far out in the surf, surge and power for the rocks. All I could do was hold the fish as hard as was sensible and let it take line if it wanted too. It turned and swam back to the left, then rushed out to sea. I played the fish closer and closer to shore. It was in front of me now, running right and left in short runs. I left the fish in the surf to tire, but waited for a bigger than average wave, and when it came, I let it lift the fish ashore. It was left, high and dry on the sand…and it was big. Phil thought it was a double, but I was less sure. We took the fish to the weigh station and there had already been a 6lb-plus bass confirmed. I watched the scales trip round and read 9lbs, 8ozs 8drs. When I gutted the fish I found chicken bones and bacon rind in the stomach. I'm guessing this fish had been feeding in nearby Bray Harbour where some yachts had been tied up. The occupants must have thrown the remnants of their dinner over the side and the bass took advantage of an easy meal.

That night, with it being late, we had to put the bass on some open beams in the low roof of the house we were staying in because there were mice running around the floor. The next night we took the bass to a restaurant and they cooked it for our party in a Hollandaise sauce, and it was delicious. Being caught on the first night of the week's competition, it was agonising waiting to see, each day, if the bass had been beaten. But it wasn't. It was the heaviest bass taken that week, and I received an inaugural, then annually given, trophy, a cheque, and a cup for the best 'bass or pollack' category. A cup I still have and will cherish forever. That second of observation through the planes window produced a lifetime's memory.

Looking back, the 80s had been good to me. I'd done what I'd set out to achieve. To gain enough experience and knowledge to reduce the percentages against me catching big bass. You have to go to the fish, they won't always come to you. What I'd also learnt was that you need to be consistent with your fishing. Take your eye of the hook for one minute and things will have changed, bringing you right back to square one.

I continued bass fishing for some years to come, but the late 80s saw me face, literally, a much bigger challenge.

Chapter 3
Shark!

"Shark!" Just the word strikes fear and panic into the heart of a human. Yet, there is also a deep fascination bordering on admiration when man is confronted by the planet's most feared predator. My first experience with a proper shark was when living in Australia, when I caught them from the shore. Bull sharks, or bronze whalers, as the Aussies call them. This awakened my desire to catch more and bigger ones, but I had to wait a while to fulfil the dream.

It was 1987. Though bass fishing was taking up much of my time, I was developing my interest in general sea fishing. As part of this broadening of personal fishing horizons, I started to fish one or two local competitions. One being what was then called the Aberystwyth Sea Angling Festival. It was while fishing the boat competition that I met John Mitchell. John was, I think, crewing on a charter boat at the time, but had the intention of getting his own boat, becoming a charter skipper, and charter fishing himself. Over time we developed a friendship and discussed, at length, the possibilities of targeting the bigger more unusual fish present in our local Cardigan Bay waters. Eventually, John bought a boat, the *Anne J*, a 36-foot steel craft with a huge open working deck. This was a boat I was to spend many happy hours on.

Gallon upon gallon of coffee was consumed by John and I long into the dark hours on many a night. The time spent swapping ideas, pouring over charts, tackle tinkering, and working out a strategy we could use to target our quarry. Porbeagles we knew were present in the bay, and sometimes, at long range over 40 miles out. Blue sharks too, with mako and even thresher having been sighted. Though not adverse to any shark taking our baits, it was the porbeagle that we decided was the shark most worthy of our attention.

John was based in Aberaeron, a little harbour town to the south of Aberystwyth, but perfectly placed for what we had in mind. I remember spending numerous nights building wire traces, stripping and servicing reels, loading the reels with new line, making up rope tailors, and a hundred other jobs in preparation for that much-longed-for first trip. The plan was to head out 40 miles, catch enough mackerel to get a good scent lane going to attract the sharks, then drift as the current took us. The first trip proved a little different though.

We headed out, on our inaugural trip, on the 19th August 1987, leaving the snug harbour and its warm lights at 2.20am. It was a small neap tide. The weather forecast was fairly settled, but with a suggestion the wind would pick up later that afternoon. John had a couple of friends aboard that day, including Colin Albert from Aberystwyth. Colin had crewed on the charter boats out of Aberystwyth since a schoolboy, had caught one small shark previously and he was as keen as mustard. Colin and I hit it off straight away and you'll hear more of Colin in future pages.

On the way out Colin and I set about mincing up fresh mackerel, then put these in to a plastic bin that was half full of animal feed bran. I then added a good pint or more of pilchard oil and mixed it all up leaving it to soak for the next hour or so. This is what the Americans call chum, and we in the UK sometimes call rubby dubby. By the time we arrived on station, had the other lads fishing and happy, Colin and I put some of the now well brewed chum in to double onion sacks and hung one off each stern corner, and one amidships on the uptide side so that the smell would be spread wider passing under the hull of the boat. We watched as the natural oil slick calmed the seas surface and spread out advertising our presence.

Putting the balloon over the side, I let it drift off with the tide about 50 yards, well out of harm's way for the lads fishing. The bait was set at about 45 feet, a whole mackerel presented head down with the hook in the head aiming to get the shark to take the hook as it initially ate the bait. The wind was against the tide, meaning the boat's drift would be slower and the chum would stay close to the boat and go fairly deep, so at 45 feet depth, I was hoping an approaching shark, lifting up through the water column as it searched for the source of the smell, would see the bait.

The ground fishing only produced dogfish and whiting, and I had a spurdog about 10lbs. It was a little after 13.40 hours. I'd been watching the balloon all the time, though my reel was on click with a very light drag set. I can't explain it, but I felt the atmosphere change. I just knew something was about to happen. I was watching the red balloon gently sway on the surface. Without hesitation it shot sideways a few feet and disappeared. The reel slowly clicked in to life, then screamed as whatever had taken the bait swam off at speed.

Picking up the rod, I let line peel off the reel for a few seconds, disengaged the clicker, eased up the drag, and felt the weight of the fish pull the rod hard over. The shark felt the resistance and charged off fast and without changing direction. It slowed, ran again, paused and ran some more, then went deep. I'd had big tope and conger prior to this, but nothing in the same league as what was on the end of my line now. Head down, head shaking, and making short, powerful runs. I kept the rod pressure hard on, the tip bent over and the 30lb line singing under the strain. The shark came up, made one more fast run, then showed itself on the surface, defiant fin out of the water. It was a porbeagle!

The fish sulked under the boat and made short bursts for freedom, but it was spent. I brought the shark to the side of the boat and John and Colin lifted it aboard. My first porbeagle, but really just a pup at 70lbs. To get our first porgie on our first trip was exciting. We wanted more!

Just a month later we headed out again, just John and I, leaving the quay at midnight and punching some 30 miles or so out in to a very calm Irish Sea. John caught a 60lber just as first light was breaking. We had nothing then until just before lunch when I boated another 70lber, followed at 14.50 by another porbeagle we estimated by length and girth to weigh around 90lbs. To say I was now obsessed with sharks would have been a massive understatement.

My next battle with a porbeagle was, unexpectedly, the following June when fishing from a small boat I shared. I was some eight miles off Barmouth in a flat sea fishing for tope. We were hitting tope to 40lbs in good numbers casting baits uptide. Now tope can run fast, and make a reel scream, when they initially take the bait, but whatever had just picked up my mackerel fillet made the tope look slow. Obviously a porbeagle, I remember just managing to turn the fish after the second run with maybe only about 30yards of 18lb line left on an ABU 7000C reel. This was a long fight on the relatively light line, but I got the fish to the boat side. We measured and girthed it in the water as best we could, for we could not bring such a big and still powerful shark in to the small boat. Our estimate was about 140lbs based on a proven mathematical formula used to measure sharks. I had a shark trace with me and immediately set up a 20lb class boat rod with a whole mackerel on under a balloon at about 25 feet, roughly mid depth. Within 20 minutes we had another shark show on the surface, which dived and took the bait. I fought it for a few minutes, then it came round in a wide circle and its fin broke surface about 40 yards off the stern of the boat, I saw, and felt, the line run up, over, and ping off the tip of the fin. The line broke just a minute or so later due to that abrasion. It was not as big as the first shark though.

A BARRIER BROKEN AND A RECORD SET

While fishing with John Mitchell, we had, many times, spoken of the chance of breaking the Welsh porbeagle record. Though porbeagle, at that time, had been caught inside Cardigan Bay for over 50 years, mostly as an accidental catch, but some also intentionally, fish over 160lbs seemed to elude those hunting them. By the late 1980s the record was still sat at 194lbs. The 200lb barrier seemed impossible to beat.

Though a rational person by nature, I've come, via many life experiences, to believe in fate. As a 16-year-old, my dad was working in a garage in Tywyn, mid Wales. Working with him, as a spray painter, was a young lad, just a couple of years older than me, who was to play a major part in a future shark adventure. His name is Charlie Bartlett. Charlie was to become one of the very best charter-fishing skippers in the whole of the UK. At the time of writing, he still is. His interests were mainly fishing and shooting, so we hit it off from the outset, and we fished together numerous times for bass until I left to live in Australia.

By the time I arrived home, Charlie was establishing his charter business with a 27-foot boat, the *Ceffyl Mor*, based in Aberdovey. Naturally I went out fishing with him, and during the late 1980s, through Charlie, I had the opportunity to join a group of anglers from Derby and Nottingham who wanted to fish for porbeagles. Amongst that group was Derby angler John Mears, who already had the record 194lb porbeagle. Charlie had built a reputation for big catches of porbeagles and with a new record recently set, confidence was high that another record would be taken sooner rather than later.

It was the first week of July, 1989. As a group, we had booked a full five days aboard the Ceffyl Mor. The forecast was light easterly winds for the first four days, with the last day looking like the wind would swing westerly and pick up to a fresh force 6. Monday the 3rd, the sea was flat as a mirror. We ran a big rubby dubby trail, but had no runs and saw no shark all day. Mackerel were scarce for bait too.

Tuesday the 4th dawned much the same with a calm sea and the air near still. It was hot and sunny. We stopped for mackerel bait by Aberdovey outer buoy, usually a prolific area for them, but not so this time. We tried various other spots as we travelled northwest out to sea, but only succeeded in getting less than a dozen. Charlie had foreseen this and ordered a box of frozen jumbo mackerel from a supplier. These would have to do for both the rubby dubby, and the hook baits. The discussion on board was that if the mackerel were not there, with little food available, it was likely the sharks would be elsewhere too. But fishing is never quite as simple as that!

There were six of us fishing. I tackled up with a 30lb class rod, and a now iconic Penn Senator 6/0 reel loaded with 28lb monofilament line. I made my own shark traces with a 4/0 sized big-game swivel at the top to tie the main line to, then 10 feet of 400lb 49-strand big game wire with a loop and another 4/0 swivel crimped in at the remaining end. Having the second swivel in place meant, if need be, I could easily change the lower section of wire if it became kinked, or damaged while fishing. To the lower swivel I crimped on five feet of 400lb 49-strand wire ending in a size 12/0 Mustad Sea Demon hook. At the time the definitive hook for shark fishing was a Mustad Seamaster. A good hook that caught many very big fish, but this pattern had a hook point offset to the shank of the hook. I'd seen porbeagles take a bait presented on a Sea Master, run, fight for a good ten minutes or more, then simply spit out the bait suggesting they had never been fully hooked in the first place. It was obvious that the offset point was not getting a full and proper grip in the mouth due to less pressure being applied to the hook point. The is why I chose the Sea Demon pattern hook with a point inline with the shank, thus applying maximum line and rod pressure directly to the hook point for maximum penetration. This was to prove relevant this very day.

With the rubby dubby slick now working well and drifting far and wide downtide, we settled in to fish with six garishly coloured balloons suspending mackerel baits at different depths from about 70 feet at the furthest, to just 20 feet down right by the stern of the boat. The middle baits being some 30 to 50 feet deep. This staggered approach means the baits should be inside the slick as it sinks like a torch beam away from the boat, with the sharks coming in at different depths at least likely to encounter one bait.

The morning passed uneventfully, time absorbed by a little bottom fishing for whiting, dabs, gurnards and rays, but most focus was on the balloons. At 2pm, as the tide picked up speed, a reel suddenly chattered as line peeled off the spool. It was John Mears' rod. It was a lively fish, but soon after setting the hook he said it was not big and duly landed a porgie about 65lbs in weight, which was instantly released. Over the next two hours there were three more shark runs. Two dropped the bait when the angler struck, and the other spat the bait after a five-minute fight. All three were using Sea Master hooks with an offset point.

At 4pm Charlie said, "Another hour lads, and its time for home. Make it count!" It was now just before 5pm and Charlie was already tidying and securing the boat for the journey home. Someone suddenly shouted, "Shark", and we looked towards the balloons. A big, black fin was cutting the surface water just rear

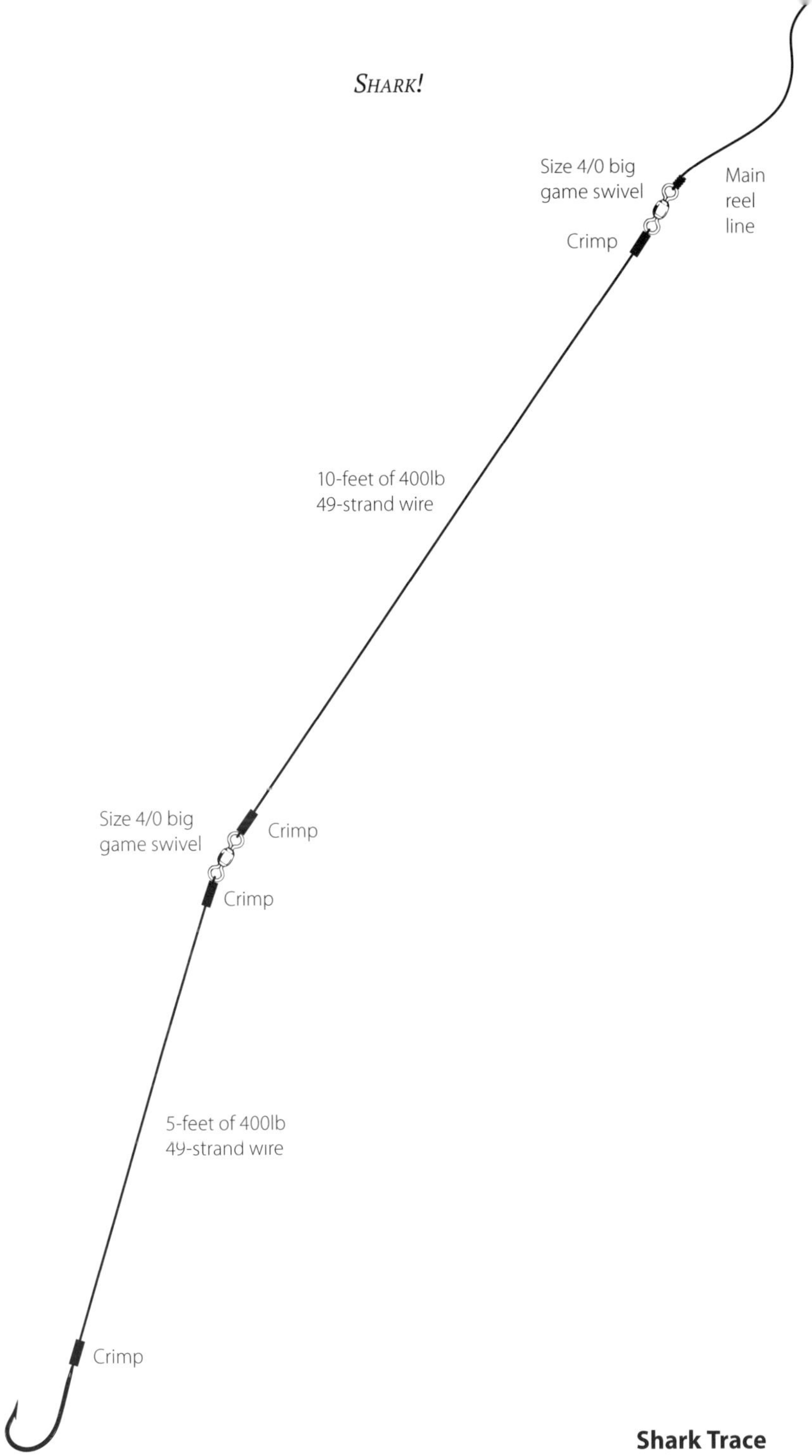
Size 4/0 big
game swivel
Main
reel
line
Crimp
10-feet of 400lb
49-strand wire
Size 4/0 big
game swivel
Crimp
Crimp
5-feet of 400lb
49-strand wire
Crimp

Shark Trace

of the furthest balloon. Before it reached that balloon it dived and we all expected one of the longer-range balloons to go at any time. A minute passed and nothing. Had the shark lost interest and was now heading for pastures new?

My balloon was closest to the stern of the boat on the port side, just 20 yards out and set to fish the bait at about 25 feet. It was a bright yellow party balloon that lazily rolled with the light sea swell, its reflection shimmering in the surface film. All eyes were on the distant balloons, but I was watching my own balloon when I saw it shudder, shoot sideways a couple of feet, then disappear vertically under water with the reel ratchet bursting in to life as the fish slowly took line. Charlie was barking instructions to the other lads to try and get their lines clear of mine. The shark ran about 50 yards, then surprisingly slowed down to a much more sedate pace. I took the decision to strike early so as not to deep hook the shark. Flicking off the ratchet and increasing the drag, I felt the rod tip pull over in to its full fighting curve and let the rod pressure set the hook. The shark felt it too and corkscrewed for the seabed taking a steep angle of descent and ripping another 75 yards of line off the reel. As the shark levelled out I got the feeling, through the rod, something did not feel right. This fish was ultra powerful and was hitting the rod tip repeatedly hard. It was uncontrollable and did not feel as it should during the fight.

An hour went by, the shark making repeatedly long runs. Two hours in and the fight was the same. Charlie came to my side and said he'd never seen a fight like this. I suggested to him I thought that when the shark corkscrewed in the early stages of the fight, that it had wrapped its tail around the trace and I was fighting it backwards. This meant I took all the strain and the fish barely knew it was hooked. Charlie had to call the Coastguard to alert them to the fact we were fighting a big fish and would be late in. After nearly three hours I got the shakes from keeping maximum strain on the fish for those initial hours. I worked through that and settled back to battling the shark. My shoulders were aching, my arm muscles stiff and sore, and my back near breaking. It kept running through my mind just exactly what was I fighting here as I'd never experienced anything like this myself either.

After four hours the shark stopped running, but went deep right down to the seabed and used its weight to hang in the tide. This is the most gruelling part for the angler. You have no choice but to bend at the knees and lean backwards to better support yourself and keep the point of balance pressure on the fish. Slowly, but very slowly, the weight was coming up, inch by hard-fought inch. I got it to mid water, but it turned and went back to the bottom. More heavy pressure saw the shark lift in the water, then I felt it roll, and a horrible sensation of line rubbing on something and pinging off came through to my hands. For a split second I thought the fish was gone, but then the weight came again and now the fight was more normal. I could lead the shark and control it with the rod. My guess that the shark had rolled in the trace looked to be correct. The shark was close to the boat now. The trace swivel came up and Charlie grabbed the trace and led the fish to surface. It was big, but not as big as the arduous fight suggested. A rope noose went round the tail and the shark was lifted aboard. John Mears and Charlie both said it looked bigger than the previous record and the decision was made to claim that record, so the fish had to be taken in and weighed properly on accredited scales. The fight lasted over five hours, and for over four hours I'd fought the fish tail first.

Back at the quay, as dark was falling, the porbeagle was weighed at exactly 205lbs. It was duly ratified as a new Welsh record, but was also the first ever fish over 200lbs of any species to be caught on rod and line in Welsh waters. In the years to come I boated much bigger sharks and other fish, in less than an hour. The circumstances with the 205lber were unique, as so often a weight barrier or record fish proves to be. So easily, when tail wrapped, the sharks tail could have touched the main line and it would have been gone. Lady Luck was with me that day, and I'm the first to realise it.

Times were different then, which is why we chose to bring the shark home for weighing and ratification. Even on the day I felt a pang of guilt, and now more so to this day, that the fish was killed. The other side to the argument, at that time, was that as a record size increased, so too did the specimen fish weight anglers use to judge a big fish, in turn helping to preserve fish below that specimen size. It was the last shark I ever chose to bring home. From that day to this all the sharks and big fish I've caught have been returned to the water alive, and more often that not, tagged to provide future information should they ever be caught again.

I continued to fish porbeagles for some years to come, and still do today, but I was about to transfer my adventures to another shark, *Prionace glauca*, the oceanic blue.

Mike's 205lb Welsh record porbeagle shark.

Chapter 4
Big Bold Blues

In the September of 1989, Colin Albert and I booked a week's holiday near Union Hall in County Cork, Ireland. We would be hiring a small 22-foot open boat with an inboard diesel engine and have the freedom to fish for whatever we liked. We spent the weeks before, as I still do to this day whenever I head for somewhere new, studying charts and ground feature, gathering information from books and relevant fishing articles on the area, and getting as clear a picture as possible as to what might be resident there. Our main fear was the weather. As the trip grew nearer the weather settled and high pressure came in a couple of weeks before we were due to go.

After a huge steak dinner at Col's we headed for the ferry at Fishguard in Col's slightly ageing Ford Escort. We were loaded for grizzly with just about every conceivable bit of tackle we owned somehow rammed in to the car with clothes, as an afterthought, stuffed in on top. The Escort looked well down-at-heel. In fact, as we travelled the road from Rosslare to Union Hall, several times the sump touched the road and we winced, but kept on going. When we got to our destination the road was steep, and such was the load in the car, the sump fully bottomed out on the tarmac and we were concerned we might do serious damage. I had to get out of the car to help lighten the weight, and Colin gently coax the car up on to the steep road, me get back in, and then we gently motored up to the house.

On meeting the owner, the caravan we were supposed to be renting had been double booked, but no worry, he said we could have the flat built on to the house. What the owner didn't tell us was that the flat was only half built with one window held in with external angled wooden braces, the walls were unplastered, and with the smallest shower and toilet unit I've ever seen. We were young, keen to fish, so readily agreed to the primitive conditions knowing full well we'd be fishing most of the time anyway. That night, we learned that the high-pressure weather system was to remain sitting over us for virtually the whole week. Great from the fishing point of view, but also useful given the gaping open edges where the flat's windows didn't fit the walls.

We were introduced to our boat. Given the state of the accommodation, I was worried the boat might be in similar shape, but thankfully it was well maintained, the diesel engine had the nice diesely 'knock' my Dad had taught me all good diesel engines should have, and there was an anchor (but not much rope) and a basic flashing light sounder. We wanted to fish a fair way out given the weather forecast and target the blue sharks. The average depth we were likely to fish out of Union Hall was no more than 300 feet, but the anchor rope was only about that in length and not enough as we wanted to anchor for the blues. I asked the owner if we could have some more anchor rope. He said, "How much, and what for?", and nearly fell off the quay when I said, "Another 600 feet, please. We want to anchor up out there. He thought I was nuts, but duly found me another 600 feet of rope.

With the weather set fair and the sea flat, the first day, the 3rd of September, we steamed out, past the Stag Rocks, about six miles in to 250 feet of water. It was a medium sized spring tide and we decided to drift fish to cover more ground. We struggled to find mackerel for bait, but caught just enough to get a bag of rubby dubby over the side putting out a scent trail, and kept four mackerel for bait, along with a few pollack we'd caught. We put a balloon out each, then fished the bottom to see what was about. Colin was quickly in with a small blue about 30lbs, and I lost one right under the boat. I also set up a second rod on heavy gear with a wire trace and two 12/0 hooks one above the other. For bait I used, literally, a 4lb pollack. This was sent vertically down, with a weight attached, to fish the bait about 40 feet above the seabed.

We were fishing feathers unsuccessfully to get more mackerel for bait, and to make room I was at the bow of the boat. Out of the corner of my eye, I saw something. A huge shark fin was coming straight at us. It was almost heading for the bow, but moved slightly to the side and approached just off the starboard side. It was the biggest porbeagle I've ever seen. Given the passage of time, I can only really rely on my diary notes made that same night, but at the time I estimated the fish to be about 10 feet in length, heavily barrel bellied, and probably around 500lbs in weight. She passed by me literally almost within touching distance and I looked right in to her lifeless black eye. I can also remember shouting to Colin and seeing his jaw drop as he saw the fish. She cruised past us, still on the surface, then dived. We were both by our rods expecting one to go at any time. The fin came up again way behind the balloons and was heading back in towards us. She dived, right by the furthest balloon, but was not to be seen again. Exactly what we would have done if we'd hooked that fish, I have no idea, but we'd have had a damn good try.

Just a couple of hours later, in mid afternoon, I had the most unbelievable take on the big pollack, which was still down there. The reel screamed and line was just ripping off. I let the fish run, picked up the rod as it slowed, pushed the drag up and felt an enormous weight. Whatever was down there, pulled back by head shaking, then spat the bait. When I retrieved the trace all that was left was the head and gill covers of the pollack. The rest had gone. How the fish missed the two hooks I have no idea. My guess is that it was a six-gilled shark.

The second day we ground fished and found the wreck of the *Kowloon Bridge* taking pollack to double figures, ling, conger to 20lbs and Colin had a specimen spotted ray. The third day we decided to go for the blues again, but this time, we intended to anchor. Our reasoning being that we wanted to get a good slick going and use the outgoing tide to carry our chum slick out in the open Atlantic in the general direction of the Fastnet Rock. We found 170 feet of water over a contour line and let the anchor go. We'd worry about hauling it in by hand at the end of the day. The sea was flat, a baking sun shone from the heavens, and all seemed right with the world. What came next was amazing!

It took only 20 minutes for the first blue shark to appear. Its indigo blue back and sweeping tail seen about 20 feet down investigating the hull of the boat. Our baits were set deeper than this, so we brought them up higher, but the blue was uninterested. It was soon joined by another, then a third. None showed any real interest in the baits. Why? They stayed with us for a half hour then they disappeared.

We added fresh mackerel to the chum bag. Instantly you could see the slick thicken with oil sitting on the surface. We'd also mixed in bran, pilchard oil, and a little sand to get the scent to drop deeper. I started to drop small chunks of mackerel in to the water too, these then sinking deeper than the scent trail and hopefully finding any sharks working very deep. This worked and within half an hour we had two blues home in on us at once. Colin caught a 65lber, and I lost a fish about the same size that spat the bait again. Then, without warning, there were blue sharks everywhere. Fins were on the surface behind the boat, with others clearly seen swimming just below the boat in the gin clear water. It was an amazing sight. We tried to count them when they were heaviest in number and we think it was about 15 fish. I found that by shaking the chum bag to give a sudden burst of scent, then dropping my bait in to the water, a seemingly disinterested blue would turn and then investigate the bait. I caught a small 30lber, then had two in quick succession, both about 70lbs. I also had to lift the chum bag out of the water as blues came in trying to eat it. But as quick as they arrived, they disappeared. We spent the rest of the day catching garfish on float tackle.

The following day we were fishing the ground out from the *Kowloon Bridge* wreck when we spotted a big erect shark fin sitting on the surface. We motored towards it slowly. I had a good look at this fin and there was no white spot at the rear of the dorsal, so it was not a porbeagle, nor was it a blue. I'm also used to seeing basking sharks *etc*, but this was none of those. My gut instinct is that it was a mako, and since then there have been mako seen and caught in this area.

BACK TO UNION HALL

I've fished blue sharks a lot over the years, but always on light 20lb class, or 12lb class tackle. Blues fight, but are not in the same league as porbeagles. A good progression for any angler looking to gain experience with big fish is to first target tope. These weigh, on average, between 20lbs and 40lbs, with blue shark weighing, again on average, 40lbs to 80lbs. Porbeagles are usually bigger than this and will usually weigh 100lbs or more. Tope fight well making short, fast runs, blues fight harder on light tackle making runs and going deep, but the porbeagle is way in front of both of them regards power, stamina, speed and obviously size, and with the ability to use every tactic in the book.

After that first trip to Union Hall, I've caught blue sharks many times since, off Cobh and Kinsale, County Cork, off Mayo, and out from Downings and Killybegs in Donegal. I've also caught them off the Cornish and Devon coast. Strangely though, I'd never returned to Union Hall until the July of 2014. I was due to work compiling fishing features in the Clonakilty area of west Cork with at least one day out with a skipper called Tom Collins who runs the *Loch An Lasc* from Reen Pier, the very pier Colin and I headed out from all those years before.

Again the day dawned hot and sunny, still, with a near flat sea, just the roll of the open Atlantic lifting the boat then slowly dropping it down like an old elevator. We were after blue sharks once more, and I was fishing with two Dublin anglers, and Mike Hennessy from Inland Fisheries Ireland, a Sea Angling Information Officer; again, Mike is someone you will come across more as these pages unfold.

Tom settled us in some 370 feet of water, some 21 miles out. He quickly put two big bags of chum over the side and we settled in to fish. The two lads fishing with us were set up at the stern of the boat on the port corner, and to give them room I went to fish up by the cabin in the walkway up to the bow. I noticed the lads were fishing quite shallow, maybe less than 30 feet deep and no more than 35 yards from the boat, so I deliberately went out double that distance over 80 yards, and so the baits were well spread, set mine at about 60 feet. This to cover more options.

It took about 20 minutes for the first shark to find us and both the Dublin lads had a fish in quick succession, both about 70lbs. Nice fish! I left my bait deep, but was already thinking that it might be too deep with the first two fish coming shallow. I waited about 15 minutes, brought my gear in, re-baited, reset the balloon to fish the bait at 30 feet and trickled the bait back out to the 80 yard mark. Within ten minutes my ratchet clicked, then sang as a blue made off with the bait. I set the hook and enjoyed a spirited fight with a nice fish we estimated to be about 90lbs. The other two lads were almost straight away in to more blues ranging from 40lbs to 80lbs.

I put a fresh bait out and while the bait was still trotting back in to position I watched the balloon skid sideways on the surface, shudder, then sink away at angle as another blue took. I only fish 8/0 hooks for blues on light tackle, so I hit the fish early as soon as they start to run fast with intent. I tend to hook my fish either in the scissors of the jaw, or in the upper lip making release much easier. I also only use bronzed hooks which will rot away pretty quickly should a shark be inadvertently lost. This fish seemed bigger and fought hard first running, then going deep. It came up stopping just shy of the surface. It swam steadily towards the port side of the bow. The rod was bent hard over one second, then I felt a tap and the fish was gone. I found the main line had been cut just above the swivel on the wire trace. Sometimes, if there is any glint, reflection or shine off a swivel, another nearby shark will attack the flash and this is what I think occurred here. It's wise to always use black nickel swivels, and when the colour comes off them with use, change them for new ones. It's a good tip I've learnt the hard way.

The lads continued to catch, while I took my time re-tackling, and I had another adventure inbetween, which I'll relate to later on in another chapter, which took up a fair chunk of time. Hennessy was fishing the bottom trying for rare rod and line hake, but to no avail. When ready I dropped my bait over the side and trickled the bait back in to position about 75 yards out. The balloon barely had time to settle again skidding off to the side and instantly disappearing. Let the fish run, wait until it fully has the bait, push the drag lever forward and wait for the line to pull tight and set the hook. I'm restrained yet excited every time this happens, for you never know what you might hook when shark fishing.

This fish fought differently. Not only did it run, but it stayed near the surface making three fast runs, then went down deep, by the looks of the reel probably 200 feet down. It sulked down there using its weight to put pressure on me and going round and round in small circles. Then it changed tactics and started to swim clockwise coming towards the bow of the boat with me scrambling up on to the bow, passing the rod underneath the anchor rope, then fighting it down the starboard side to the stern. The fish sulked briefly then resumed the clockwise navigation. It often happens but this fish took me round the bow again and down the starboard side, then shot off and sulked. I piled on the pressure now, the shark slowly coming up in the water as she tired.

We saw the fish maybe 30 feet-plus down in the clear Atlantic water, circling in small figure of eight shapes. I kept the fish coming, but at the stern corner, and right on the surface, the fish saw the boat, turned her head sideways and headed back for the depths dragging line off the reel at an alarming rate. She steadied about mid water, and once again turned to go clockwise. I kept the pressure on, really working the fish and deliberately gaining just a few inches of line by pumping the rod tip upwards a few inches and only retrieving line on the down stroke. This time I felt the fish tire and piled on more pressure. We'd seen the fish, so knew it was a good size. It came up tail twisting and body turning still trying to throw the hook. It broke surface and it did look a good fish. We lifted her aboard, measured her length and girth, tagged her with an Irish Fisheries tag, and released her to grow on. The length and girth suggested a fish in excess of 120lbs, and that, even after all these years, is the biggest I've had in Irish waters. We lost count of the sharks caught that day. It was pleasing for me, having fished there for blues some 25 years previously, to return and see their numbers as good as ever, and with big fish in amongst them.

At the time of writing, the UK record blue shark of 218lbs, taken back in 1959 off Looe in Cornwall, has without doubt been broken several times, but the fish released without claiming. The Irish record, a fish caught off Achill Head in Mayo, also in 1959, has also been rocked by since-released fish. It still remains that blue shark over 100lbs in UK and Irish waters are big for the species. It used to be that to claim a specimen fish the captor had to bring the shark to shore for official weighing. Thankfully, in 2015, the Irish Specimen Fish Committee now allow a specimen blue shark to be verified by length, this being 190cms measured from the tip of the nose to the fork of the tail. If a fish is as big or bigger than this, it can be verified by the skipper of the boat, witnessed by other anglers on board, then submitted for consideration. The International Game Fish Association, while still running a heaviest weight category listing for record fish, now also have a list compiled by the length of species. This is a major move forward for angling conservation giving primarily the chance to release fish for the future, but also allowing the angler recognition for the capture of outstanding fish. Times have changed, and for the better.

We will move on from sharks now to another fish that grows to immense size that will test your reserves of determination, stamina and strength: the Giant Common Skate.

Chapter 5
Not So Common

Before commercial fishing became so intense and effective, as recent as the end of the 19th Century, the giant common skate could potentially grow to weights in excess of 500lbs. Records from these times confirm this. Even today skate can weigh in excess of 250lbs, with occasional 300lbs-plus fish landed in deeper water by commercial vessels. The fish are called 'common' because at one time that's exactly what they were, a common catch. They were found throughout the whole of the UK and Ireland, but as numbers depleted, mainly as a result of commercial overfishing (but, it has to be said, also due to poor angling practice prior to more enlightened times from the 1980s onwards), they became much more localised in their distribution.

These areas were the west coast of Scotland from Oban northwards, Scrabster, all around the Orkney Islands, and Shetland. The west coast of Ireland, especially Tralee Bay in Kerry, Clew Bay in Mayo, the Donegal coast, and the Antrim coast, also retained enough numbers of skate to maintain the overall stock level.

My first encounter with common skate was back in 1994 fishing out in Clew Bay, Ireland. I was one of a group of angling journalists asked to look at the fishing available in the bay. We were to stay at what is now the famous Helm Hotel and restaurant in Westport. I remember sitting in the bar that first night and being fascinated by the black and white photos of giant common skate hanging on the walls that had been caught there back in the 1950s and 1960s. Unfortunately these fish were all killed and an inevitable decline in catches followed, with few if any anglers bothering to fish for the big skate from the early 1970s through until the early 1990s. As we sat drinking and talking of these giant fish, it was still the case that little fishing was being done for them, so no one really knew at that time if the numbers of skate had declined further, were stable, or increasing. However there had been some tag and release fishing for common skate done within Clew Bay for a couple of years previously. Our mission was to first and foremost try and catch some; to help highlight their existence, and promote the chance of catching them. Also, and most importantly, any fish we caught were to be tagged and released to help the process of further understanding them and ultimately provide the knowledge to better protect them in the future.

The first of October dawned a wet, drizzly day with a low overcast sky. The forecast was for it to brighten up with maybe a hint of faint sunshine by mid afternoon. The wind was a steady force 3 to 4 and from the southwest. The tide was middle sized at 26.6-feet and in decline towards smaller neap tides. Our skipper for the day was an experienced local man, Frank Clarke, who, at the time, was pioneering the resurgence in Clew Bay skate fishing aboard his boat, *Corulan*.

As we motored out passing the many small islands (there is said to be an island for every day of the year inside Clew Bay) we were eagerly tackling up. I had decided to use a Shakespeare American built 50lb class Ugly Stik with all roller rings. A powerful rod, but with a slightly soft tip that would help cushion the power of such a potentially big fish, but with the stiffer lower section and stiff butt to give the leverage to pump the leviathan up off the seabed. The reel I chose was my ever faithful Penn Senator 6/0 loaded with 50lb mono. I'd given careful thought to the terminal tackle. This would be a simple small sliding boom on the main line with a bead butting up against a strong 4/0 sized big game swivel. To the swivel I'd crimped on a four-feet length of 250lb commercial monofilament. I decided on four-feet because I wanted the heavy mono to be long enough to protect the main line from contact with the wings and nose of the skate to safeguard from any contact with the weaker main line. The hook was a 12/0 Mustad O'Shaughnessy 3406.

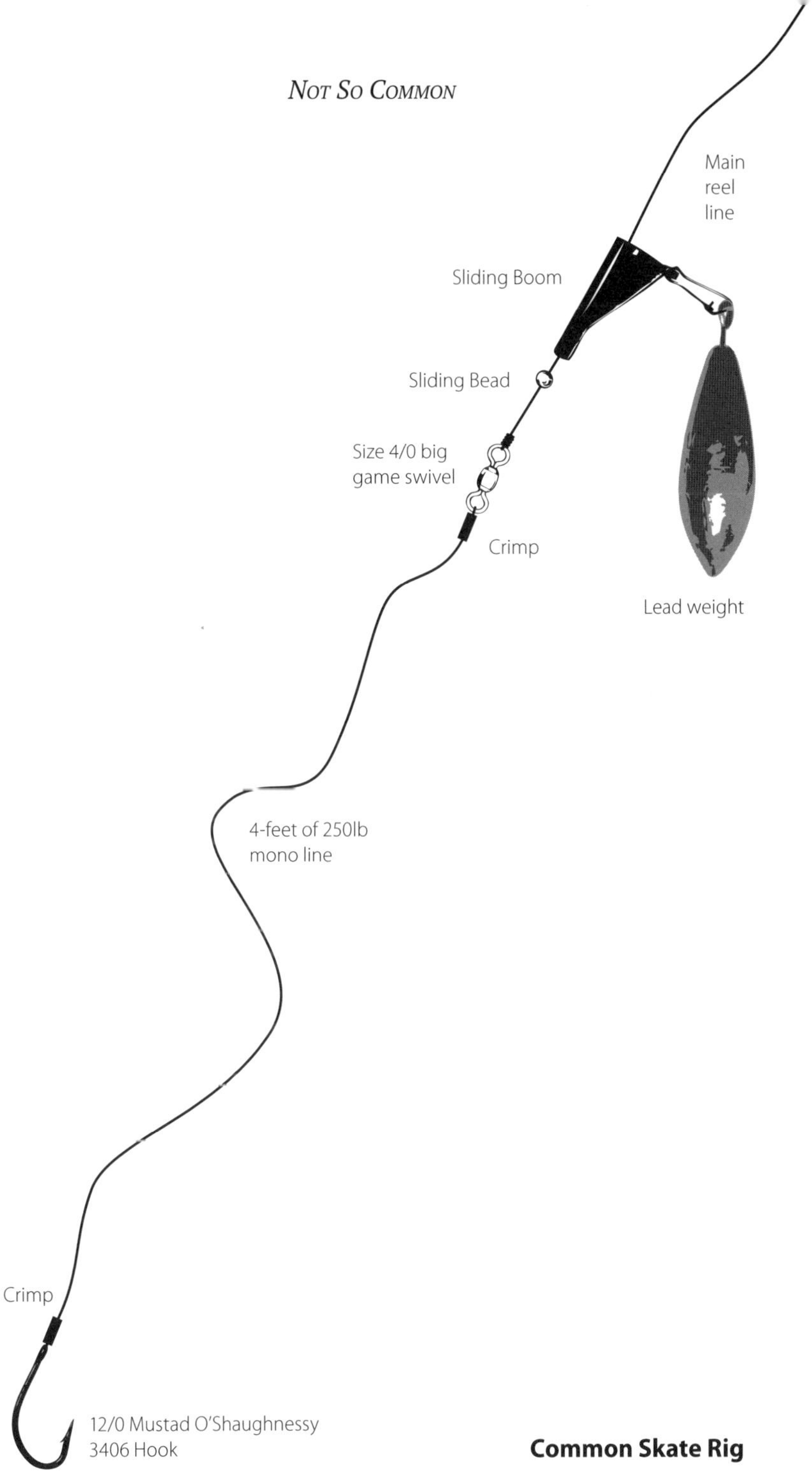

Common Skate Rig

We set anchor in just 60 feet of water close in off Inishgort Lighthouse. There was little tide run here, so I added just an 8oz lead weight to the clip on the boom via a short length of weaker line that would allow the weight to break free should it become snagged. This 8oz weight would ensure it was heavy enough to keep the bait on the seabed, but would be easily dragged across the seabed if the boat swung at anchor in the wind. Baits were going to be a mix of mackerel flappers (mackerel with the fillets left attached to the head but with the backbone cut out), or the head and half body of a dogfish with the entrails still attached. There were six of us fishing on the day and included Norman Dunlop, a Sea Angling Advisor with the Fisheries Board based in Dublin and someone, further in the future, I was to share many Irish adventures with.

There was little activity until just after low water when a rod at the stern bumped a couple of times and the ratchet gave line. The fish spat the bait. However within a few minutes another rod started to click as it also gave line. The angler picked up the rod, braced himself, and the rod buckled over in to an impressive curve. It took him over an hour to land the fish. It was estimated to weigh in excess of 150lbs and was likely to have been the fish that spat the bait just prior to being hooked. Norman was next in with a fish about the same size, but Norman, a highly skilled angler, had the fish to the boat side in under 50 minutes. Both fish caught had already been previously tagged proving the fact that these fish tend to be very much localised, but also that catch, tag and release does no long term harm. Two more fish were then lost in quick succession and I was wondering if my turn would ever come.

I was positioned just above the port side stern corner and I'd changed the way I'd baited up. The other anglers were all using flapper mackerel hooked through the two jaws with the fillets left hanging loose. I'd noticed that when the three fish had been lost, that the hooks came back with just the head of the mackerel left and the fillets completely gone. This was *deja vu* for me having had similar experiences with shark, so I chose to cut off the tail fin of the mackerel, thread the hook down the length of the mackerel in and out stitching style, and bring the hook point eventually out just above the gill cover. This would force the skate to take the bait from the head end and take the hook fully in. I also stabbed the mackerel with a knife point to help release more scent.

It was now a little after 2pm with the tide starting to flood, and as forecast a gentle hazy sun was trying to break through the heavy ceiling of thick, almost oppressive, cloud. The cloud was also lifting off the mountains. To the east I could now make out the faint shape of Croagh Patrick, known locally as 'The Reek', emerging from the gloom of the earlier day. I was taking in the scenery, when, out the corner of my eye, I saw a gentle shudder on the rod tip. There it was again, and again, then nothing. I was almost convinced it was just a small whiting ripping at the big bait, when the rod tip gently pulled over and my reel began to methodically tick as line trickled off the spool. I waited for about 30 seconds on the advice of Frank before picking up the rod, tightening the drag, leaning back by bending my knees and braced myself simply letting the fish pull the rod hard over to set the hook.

A tremendous weight was felt below and, through the rod, I felt the giant skate flap its wings and turn downtide still ticking line off slow and sure. The rod was bent right to the butt and I now realised I wasn't wearing a butt pad. Asking for one, one of the other lads buckled the butt pad around my waist and I settled in to what was likely to be a long fight. The fish had gone to ground now, just using its weight and width of wing to suction to the seabed. The only thing to do is to keep that rod bent. It is a war of attrition, the one with the most will power and endurance will win.

I've since learnt that it takes about 15 minutes to get a 150lb skate up off the seabed, and about another five minutes per 50lbs of skate weight to move a bigger fish. During the initial 15 minutes or so when you are trying to lift this denizen of the deep, your back starts to ache. First in the small of the back, then it spreads to the shoulders and neck. Your arms, kept rigid and tense holding the rod, hurt in the muscle, and your legs start to tighten in the thighs as the constant, almost overbearing, pressure takes its toll. This was a new experience for me with only some of the skills I'd learnt fighting big shark being applicable.

After keeping the rod bent under heavy pressure for a little more than 15 minutes, I felt the fish stir and flap away a few feet. As it did so I pumped the massive weight below as hard as I could up off the seabed a few feet. The fish swung towards me then hung in the water. It took a few feet of line off the reel, then came upwards a little more. This is how it was until the fish was maybe 30 feet above the seabed, then I felt it turn its head and flap back down dragging line off the reel and making me hold on trying hard not to let the fish reach the seabed. Luckily the fish levelled off above the bottom, but again dragged line off the reel as it flapped its wings heading downtide. It hung in the water, a massive weight, just going nowhere. I pumped the rod in short upwards jerks, this designed to retrieve precious inches of line at a time, always gaining on the fish forcing it higher and higher in the water by little increments. I remember brushing sweat off my brow, and that my hair was wet with sweat on top, and at the back.

It was now a give-and-take battle. I would win a few feet, the skate would take it back. I felt though, that the fish was weakening, so I upped the pressure on the fish and worked the rod hard giving the fish no time to rebalance. The line had been at a slight angle away from the boat during the early fight, but was now vertical below the rod tip. I knew I had to keep the fish's head up and coming towards me. The fish, now going round in tight clockwise circles, was getting close. The others, crowded at the stern peering in to the murky depths. Suddenly they as one burst in to a babbling chorus that I assume meant they could see the fish. A couple of minutes later I too caught a brief glimpse of a giant fawn-coloured back swinging in to view. Skipper Frank and his crewman Tom were on hand with gaffs. My job now was to lead the fish in nose-first towards them, and on the surface, so they could carefully place the gaffs in the leading edges of the wings where it does no harm. I watched, shaking with a mixture of fatigue, excitement and fear, should the fish now be lost. With two quick strokes of the gaffs the boys braced themselves and I watched open-mouthed as this huge skate was slid on to the deck, almost prehistoric in looks, but one of the most beautiful creatures I'd ever witnessed. It was also a new skate not previously tagged and may have only just recently come in to Clew Bay waters from the deeper water west of Clare Island.

The fish was measured for length and width, and Frank estimated the fish to weigh in the region of 170lbs. The weight did not matter much. To me it was the privilege to catch such a monster. After tagging and a few photos, the skate was lifted gently to the side and I watched it slide safely back in to the sea, and after sinking for just a few seconds, its wings beat in to life and we watched its defined shape blur, the colour fade to a just a pin-prick, then it was gone, but forever etched in to my memory. There was another skate about the same size as my own taken within 20 minutes of mine being released, another fish about 170lbs.

That was the only time I've fished common skate in Ireland. It is good to report that the common skate were kept off the Irish specimen list with all fish tagged and released. The fishery, as a consequence, has witnessed a healthy increase in the numbers of skate that now reside off the Irish coast, with evidence that they are once again repopulating their old haunts, and this, in turn, will have a spill on effect elsewhere. The numbers of anglers interested in catching these giants of the deep has also grown proportionately, and The Helm Restaurant in Westport has run a successful annual skate festival in October for many years.

THE SKATE OF SCAPA FLOW

In 2003 I was asked to undertake some angling survey work in Orkney. My brief was to survey the sea fishing as it was at the time, form conclusions as to how best future angling promotion could be targeted with regard to tourism, and identify any species that might be there but that were not currently fished for to add to the usually targeted species. Also to report on the facilities available to anglers regarding the boats and accommodation available, and generally look at how, and if in any way, the angling package offered in the region might be improved for the benefit of all. I've undertaken this type of work in other areas around the world, and my intention would never be, in any way, to try to belittle local anglers or charter skippers. My intention, where and if possible, is to only help improve prospects for those involved in making a living from sea angling, either in part or whole. To do this it is important to work with the local boat men and anglers as much as possible using their knowledge just as much as me relying on my own experiences to form any conclusions.

Having arrived in Orkney, literally having walked off the ferry, I was whisked in to a meeting of interested parties with at least some association with angling in Orkney. I was somewhat shocked at the time to find that some people were quite hostile to me being there. I gave a short address detailing a few of my intentions, and stating I had no intention nor interest in 'treading on toes'. One of the intentions I voiced was to look at reviving a once lucrative rod and line common skate fishery and setting in motion a tag and release programme. I was quickly told that the common skate were all gone and would never be back. I won't dwell on this unpleasant experience, but suffice to say my spirits were lifted when I also met a few people who saw the benefits of this survey and tried hard to encourage and help me towards the intended goal. However this hostility was to plague me further.

The research on Orkney, though I was already aware of it from simple pleasure reading all those years before as a boy, was that during the 1960s and in to the early 1970s some large common skate had been caught inside Scapa Flow. In fact a very famous angler, Leslie MonCrieff, who was instrumental in the design of surf casting rods and long range fishing techniques for shore fishing at the time, caught fish from the east side of the Island of Hoy inside Scapa Flow under the guidance of local skipper Frank Sinclair. There were numerous other instances of common skate being caught around Orkney too. These mostly by commercial fisherman though.

During the 1970s and 1980s commercial fishing techniques killed large numbers of these fish with them used sometimes for lobster and crab pot bait, also as simple 'dig in' fertiliser for locals, or just killed and dumped over the side. During the 1990s this continual kill dramatically reduced as commercial fishing methods changed. Delving deeply in to the situation I found that some common skate, especially around the islands to the north of mainland Orkney, were still being caught, some on long-lines and released alive. It was obvious the skate were still there, but not being caught on rod and line, simply because local skippers and anglers were not specifically targeting them.

Going back to reading the Admiralty charts, reading books for old reports, and studying tide flow and ground features around Orkney I was able, at least in part, to identify certain areas I felt common skate would still be resident. Some of these were proven when talking to commercial fisherman on the islands, who, unlike some of the angling fraternity, proved to be very helpful and interested in what we were trying to do. I had a feeling that the wrecks inside Scapa Flow would also likely be home to resident common skate that would lay up close to the structure on clean ground using the wreck to break the tide flow. The wrecks would also attract lots of small fish and therefore would prove a reliable food hunting ground for the big skate. I needed access to the wrecks. Little did I know another setback was about to present itself.

There was, and still is, a major and financially very important pleasure diving industry based in Orkney, especially in the safer waters of Scapa Flow where the German fleet rests after the mass scuttling undertaken on the 21st of June 1919 on the orders of German Admiral Ludwig von Reuter. The Admiral did not want the ships of his fleet falling in to British and allied hands. During the scuttling, some 52 of 74 ships were sunk. Some subsequently salvaged, but others lay there to this day, many being popular dive wrecks.

I knew that these same wrecks, at least a proportion of them, would also be important for future angling development, especially for conger, ling, cod, coalfish and pollack. The diving people had other ideas, even though I deliberately chose wrecks that were the least popular with divers to initially experimentally fish. This out of courtesy and to not interfere with an important industry and financial avenue already in place. However, on two occasions while trying to fish a wreck with no other vessels around, dive boats appeared and put divers straight in to the water right by me, even though there were more popular dive wrecks nearby. Given the danger of hooks in the water and the possibility of hooking divers below, I had no choice but to lift anchor and move. It was pretty obvious they did not want me there!

One wreck was suggested to me though, that could be fished,

and without fear of divers intervening. I was shocked when I learnt which it was. It was the *Royal Oak*, a war grave with no unauthorised diving allowed out of respect to those that died when she was sunk by the German submarine U-47 captained by Gunther Prien just after midnight on 14th October 1939. He brought the U-47, undetected, through a narrow and very shallow navigation passage at Kirk Sound on the east side of Scapa Flow, and torpedoed the Royal Oak. Some 834 men lost their lives that night, and the wreck is now left as reminder to the total futility of war.

I immediately refused to fish directly over the wreck out of respect to those sailors who rest there. What I decided to do was to fish around the edge of her some 100 yards away from the actual wreck and see if I could draw the fish to me. I was fortunate in having a young charter skipper, Alistair Wallbank and his boat *Charlie Says* to fish from within Scapa Flow. Alistair was a keen and enthusiastic skipper who was willing to try anything to get a result. This attitude was vital!

My first day fishing by the *Royal Oak* was the 14th July 2004. It was a rainy day with a light southwest wind. We used some of the day to assess the wreck and get an idea of how she was laying. We could then judge the tide flow and direction, and the wind, then position the boat above the wreck and use the scent from the baits to travel in towards the wreck to draw any fish out. We had instant success with ling over 12lbs and conger to 20lbs. We changed our position in relation to the wreck several times and we noticed that off to one side was an incline in the seabed. My intention the next day was to try to get the boat so positioned that I could get a bait on to the lip of the dip in the seabed. It was a hunch, but I had a feeling this dip might hold a common skate.

The 15th of July was a different day. The wind had turned in to the north, a strong, cold wind that even in July carried a hint of the ice pack about it. It also came with a persistent drizzle, the type that seems to find every little chink in your clothing armour and soaks you through. The sea, even inside Scapa Flow, was choppy with a little swell. Alistair and I worked together to get the boat in the right place, but with the wind it took us a couple of attempts to get it right. I set up using the same type of 50lb class tackle, though the reel was now a Penn International 30 lever Drag loaded with 50lb monofilament. The rig was the same sliding ledger rig system I used to catch my first Irish skate. The bait was a whole mackerel, again with the tail fin removed and the hook stitched in then positioned just to the rear of the gill cover to make a fish take the hook end.

We had been fishing for a couple of hours and so far managed only a small ling under 10lbs. I replaced the original lead weight for a much lighter one and slowly tried to work the bait a little further away from the boat by repeatedly lifting the rod and 'bouncing' the lead and bait further downtide by releasing a little line. I was trying to drop the bait in to that dip we had previously seen on the fish finder. When I thought the bait was in the right place, I put the rod in the gunnel rod tube, set the reel on a light drag with the clicker on, and went back to fishing the bottom with light tackle for smaller species.

Maybe a half hour passed, and while landing a small whiting I noticed one small pull down on the skate rod, then a pause, a shudder, then nothing. I waited...still nothing. Then I watched the line as it entered the water drop slack. Whatever was down there had picked up the bait and started to move back towards me. Picking up the rod, I just waited a moment to see what was happening. The line was slack but tightening slowly, then stopped. This was confusing. I was thinking maybe a small ray of some sort had taken the bait and was pulling the lead weight around. Slowly the line tightened, and as line started to leave the reel spool slowly and steadily, I continued to let the fish run. This was no small ray. Holding the rod and bracing myself I eased the lever drag forward to add line pressure, and as the line came fully tight the rod pulled over in to that most satisfying of arcs. The pressure pulled on my back and I instantly bent at the knees and leaned backwards to get a point of balance against the fish.

I was very conscious this fish was relatively close to the wreck, and typically that was the way it wanted to go, straight for the wreck. I piled a lot of pressure on that fish and forced it to turn. It swung downtide and went to ground. My son, Mike Jr, was onboard with me, and I whispered to him that this was a common skate. In turn, he whispered the same message to Alistair, the skipper. I did not voice my suspicions out aloud as I wanted to make sure what it was first. I kept maximum pressure on that fish and after maybe 10 minutes it moved. I 100% knew now that it was a common skate. Slowly, I felt the fish flap further downtide, but I could dictate the fight now. The fish came up in the water maybe 20 feet, then took all the line back trying to dive for the seabed. It then held in the water, sometimes swimming in a tight circle, but also making short runs of a few yards. I kept heavy pressure on and using that short upward pump of the rod tip gained a precious few inches of line as the rod dropped back each time. The fish made one more dive, then I felt it was tired and played the fish quickly to the surface. It was not the biggest skate I'd caught, but at the time it was by far the most important.

We gently lifted the skate aboard. It was a male fish, and one of the biggest male common skate I've ever seen. I also noted that this fish was much thicker and heavier in the body behind the head than others I caught in Ireland. It was obvious to me that this stock of common skate in Orkney may be the same genetic fish, but their body characteristics are different. The fish was estimated, after some discussion and measuring, to be around 130lbs. After photographs were taken, it was immediately returned to the water where it flapped its way back to the depths. It was the first confirmed and verified common skate on rod and line for probably more than 20 years according to what some of the locals said. What mattered was that we had proved the point that common skate remain a viable rod and line target for anglers visiting the Orkney Islands.

Returning to the quay in Stromness, by chance, one of the doubters from that original meeting when I was told the common skate were no longer there, was working on the quay. He came across as we walked back up the steps off the boat. He asked if we'd had any success. I said, "Yes! Would you like to see the photo?" That was the beauty of the early digital cameras, instant photos. He was visibly taken aback. I showed him the photo. He said nothing, he just turned and walked away, back to what he was doing, without a second glance.

OBAN GIANTS

The Oban area in the west of Scotland is another haven for giant common skate. Here the water is much deeper, often in excess of 500 feet. There are very big fish here with 200lb-plus fish regularly taken. It was February 2010, and we had two days booked aboard Ronnie Campbell's boat, the *Laura Dawn*. My son and I were with a group of anglers from all over the UK and Scotland, including a good friend of ours, Adam Riach from Keith, Moray, and Glaswegian angler Ewan Hill. Also with us was carp angler, Mark Cole, from the south of England. In his own words he'd "only just discovered sea fishing" and was really enjoying the diversity of species and locations, as opposed to fishing the same syndicate and day ticket waters week after week.

It was the 22nd of February. The hills had white overcoats of snow, and a cold northerly wind howled down the loch cutting through our thick layers of clothes like a knife. It was cloudy with more snow forecast for later. The tide chosen was deliberately a small neap tide just before the lowest tide of the cycle. In this deep water the bigger faster flowing tides are difficult to fish.

Ronnie chose a deep hole in some 470 feet of water. Both mackerel and half dogfish baits went down. I'd chosen not to fish for skate and would try for the spurdog and maybe, though an unlikely capture in February, a black mouthed dogfish for my species count. Only Adam and Ewan had caught a skate previously, just one each, with Mike and Mark both skate virgins, so with me having caught them before, I also wanted to give the other guys the very best chance of catching one. It was a good day. First Ewan Hill decked a 120lb male fish, followed by Adam with a bigger 155lb female. Two fish were then unluckily lost by Mike Jr after a brief fight with the hooks just simply pulling out, then Mark Cole, after a long fight, boated a superb 193lb skate. Straight away Mike Jr was hooked up again and this time boated his first ever skate, a 60lb-plus male. I'd had spurdog, but nothing big while fishing off the bottom. The other guys had all lost their skate virginity now, so the following day I figured I'd try and get another skate under my belt.

The 23rd of February was the lowest neap tide of the cycle, with high water at midday. The sun was out, but more snow had fallen overnight. The chill northerly wind was still there, but it turned easterly and freshened during the day. Skipper Ronnie chose a different venue in some 530 feet of water. Almost immediately the baits hit the seabed Adam hooked and lost a good fish. Another two fish were hooked and both came adrift again after a few minutes. Ewan Hill then hooked a fish that was obviously much bigger. This was a dogged fight, the fish sticking to the seabed for nearly 20 minutes before rod pressure took its toll. Slowly the big fish came up and on the surface it looked huge. It measured out at about 205lbs, a true monster. Adam also boated a fish that weighed in the region of 180lbs.

Inbetween these two skate, I'd put down a mackerel bait and was watching the rod tip rather than relying on the line clicker going off. As I'd done so many times before, I saw the little shudder on the rod tip. This is the wings or nose of the skate touching the line, but can also be the movement of water on the line produced as the skate flaps its wings as it gets in to position prior to settling over the bait. They can also shuffle over a bait to align it with their mouth. These register up the line on to the rod tip. Given a typical skate bite, I always wait until the fish starts to tick line off the reel, pick up the rod and let the weight of the fish bend the rod and pull the hook home. Never strike these fish in the true sense by jagging the rod tip up and down, as this is a sure way to snap the line.

I picked up the rod and, with my thumb over the free to run spool, allowed the skate to move off with the bait, then tightened the drag, bent at the knees, leaned back, and felt the weight of the fish pull the rod hard over. The fish ran maybe 25 yards, then instantly suctioned down on the seabed. I settled in to keeping the pressure hard on the fish. A quarter of an hour later it moved a few feet, then suctioned back down. Another five minutes of sweat and back-breaking pain got the fish moving. I really fought this fish hard and it came up through the water fairly quickly, but then turned back for the seabed and took a good 40 yards of line with it on this dive. Eventually it broke surface and was a good one. It was slid through the stern door of Ronnie's boat and measured out at about 175lbs. What was interesting about this fish is that it had already been caught and tagged. The tag number was 4963.

The fish was in perfect health and good condition. This proves again the point that rod and line, tag and release fishing, done properly, does not harm fish in any way and is one of the most useful forms of information collection, in regards to overall stock numbers, migration, habitat and growth of fish, that we have at our disposal.

In the two days we boated seven skate, with five over 100lbs, in addition to the 205lber. We had lost five fish after brief fights, and had several runs that did not materialise in to a hook up. Such is the life of a giant skate angler.

Tope. Often called the poor man's shark, yet they are one of the hardest fighting fish in UK waters. They are our next target!

Chapter 6
Titan Tope

I like tope. They are strong, powerful, shallow water shark that fight hard on light, balanced tackle. My home waters of Cardigan Bay in Wales is one of the UK hotspots, so consequently I've done a lot of tope fishing over the years, from both shore and boat. I served my time fishing for tope from numerous charter boats during the 1980s and 1990s, but it wasn't until I got my own boat in 1994, a 17'6" fast planing hull called *Lamna*, that I really started to target the bigger tope and think things out for myself.

I was aware of numerous big tope taken over the years inside Cardigan Bay, especially over the reef and clean ground north of Aberdovey where my friend, charter skipper Charlie Bartlett, has had more than his share of big tope in excess of 60lbs, and also a couple of 70lbers, over the gunnels of his boats through the years.

I knew the inshore reef ground very well as I'd fished it extensively for bass. Additionally, I'd caught tope in excess of 40lbs from the reef edges, often in less than 10 feet of water. There were bigger fish present on the reefs, but it always seemed to me that they were very few and far between. These usually being big females that were looking for somewhere to safely pup and in water recently vacated by the more common pack tope that run up to about 30lbs or so.

What was also intriguing was that I knew from annual catches that the tope first showed in the early April period, usually about 20 miles out around some reef ground. They would stay there for a few days, then move on to pastures new as they depleted the food supply in that area. These though were the pack tope. I had a theory that the pack tope, these being made up of both male and female tope, would have to have somewhere specific to head for when ready to breed. In turn, the big females would also move to this area to meet up with the males. I started to pour over the Admiralty charts again and, by superimposing what I knew about previous catches on to the charts, I was able to identify two spots that might produce the size of fish I wanted. By chance, a casual conversation with Charlie suggested I was on the right track, as he too had found an area that at the time I felt the tope were breeding on, and this had produced some big fish for him, with one estimated at over 70lbs.

During 1996 I experimented with the area and found that the tope moved on to a patch of sandbanks around the beginning of May. They would stay on these for about three weeks, then leave almost overnight and spread out much more thinly on the inner shallows. Mostly fishing with my regular fishing mate Clive Griffiths, also with my son, we enjoyed some great days tope fishing in the May period. Looking back through the diary our best day for numbers was a staggering 53 tope to a little over 50lbs, this fish estimated using the length and girth measurement formula. We had another day with 44 tope landed, and two more days when more than 30 tope were landed. Remember this was just with two or three people fishing.

This was the information I was looking for. If they were in peak numbers for just that three week period in the one place, this had to be the area they used for mating. This would be where the biggest females came to mate with the male pack tope. I christened the area, 'The Red Light District'.

I also gave a lot of thought to tackle. At this time there was a swing away from wire for the hook trace to heavy 200lb commercial monofilament. The idea was that it was better for the tope should a fish be inadvertently lost. However, being aware of what even a 30lb tope could do with its triangular, ultra sharp, serrated edged teeth, I had no faith in the mono and left it alone. A decent tope in the 40lb bracket, if held at the side of the boat, will thrash its head side to side. This is enough to cut through the 200lb mono, I've seen it happen many times. A bigger 50lb fish would make that cut even easier. Besides, whether you use heavy mono or wire, the weak link on the trace should a fish be lost will always be the hook. This

Boat Tope Trace

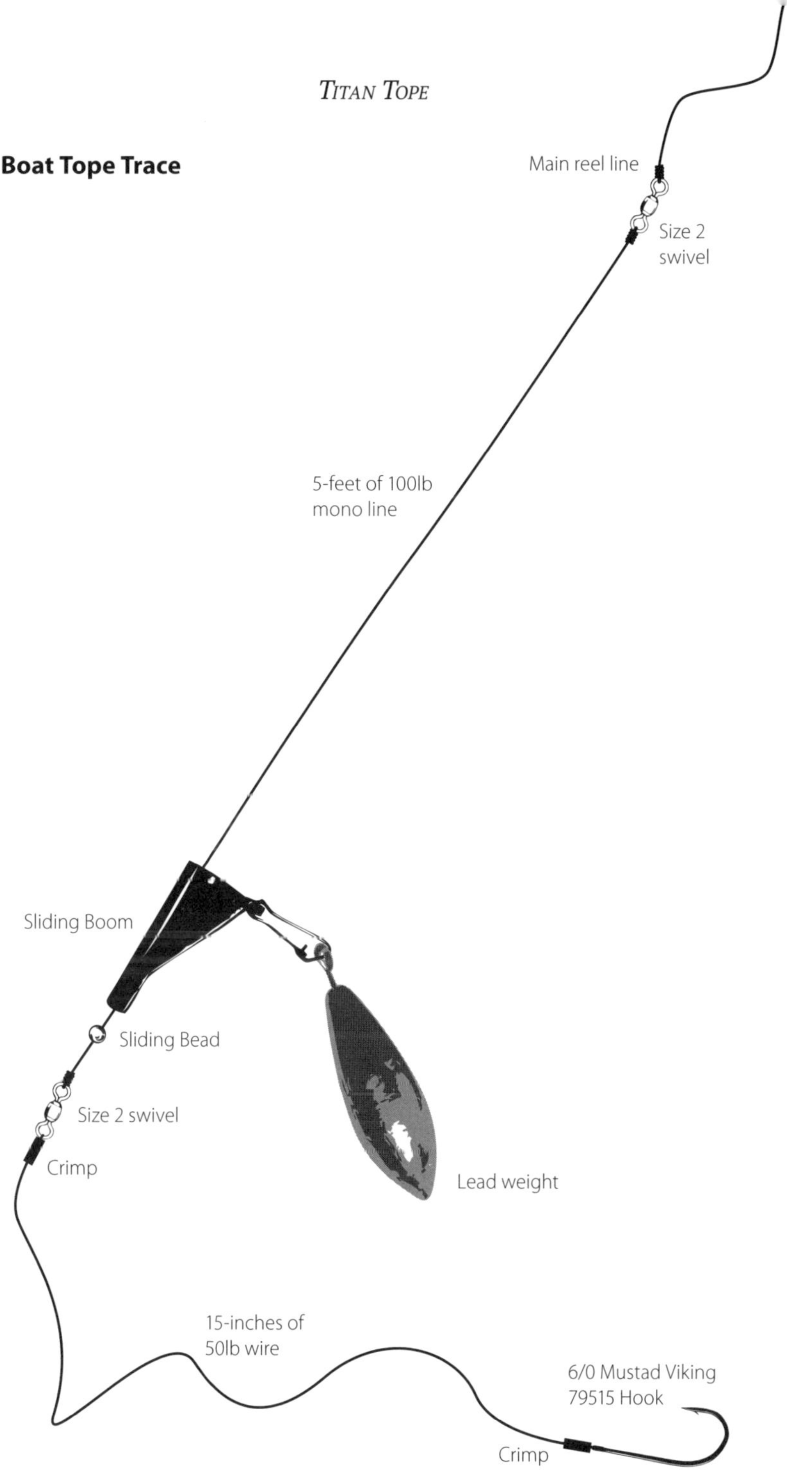

will rot out quickly if it is a bronzed pattern. Also a short section of multi-strand wire is more supple than heavy mono and does not impair a tope from feeding while the hook dissolves, which will take just a few days using that bronzed hook.

My tackle for big tope was a 9ft 6in uptide rod capable of casting 6ozs and bait with a supple tip, but quickly increasing power in the mid section feeding in to a stiff butt. At the time the best reel for the job was the ABU 7000C loaded with 18lb mono and an 80lb mono shock leader. I attached a size 2 rolling swivel to the shock leader, added five feet of 100lb mono, slid on a short sliding boom, then a 5mm bead, then tied on another swivel. To this swivel I crimped on 15 inches of 50lb multi-strand wire. Crimped to the end of the wire was a size 6/0 Mustad Viking 79515 hook, but with the barb pressed flat by pliers. This rig was strong, and had the 100lb line to minimise abrasion should a tope's body roll in the trace, or the tail catch it when swimming. If fishing near snags I would also attach the weight to the boom clip via a weak link of line that would snap if the weight jammed in stones so as not to impair the fish unduly.

This rig also had another purpose. With the weight attached to the short boom and free to slide on the 100lb mono, as a tope took the bait and swam off, the trace slid through the boom until it hit the top swivel. The lead weight naturally lifts in the water to the weight of the tope as this happens, so this acts like a bolt rig often hooking the tope in the scissors of the jaw making unhooking easy. The Mustad hook was light in the wire, but ultimately strong, and it could be honed to a knife-edge point. This meant the hook would get a good grip and sink deep without the need for overly heavy rod pressure. This ensuring better hook ups and more secure hook holds.

In April 1997 I made a couple of early tope trips, catching a few good ones to nearly 40lbs, but mostly just keeping in touch with their movements. I followed them in from the early offshore reef ground using reports from the charter boats, then on to the ground just a few miles offshore, then waited, with much anticipation, for the first ones to be caught by the charter boats on the sandbanks. When news came the tope were there, it was time to try myself.

We had a day the second week of May that produced 26 tope,

the best close to 45lbs. I had a feeling the tope were running slightly later than normal. Work and rougher seas meant the third week I could not fish. The last opportunity would be the very end of May. Work colleague and great friend Rob Wyatt was coming down from the Midlands and was due to fish with my son and myself. The forecast looked good and we were all set.

It was the 31st of May. The tide a rising 26.9-feet. I wanted to leave early, at 4.30am, and head out to the banks straight away. We launched on a bright morning that promised sunny conditions, but as is so often the case locally to me, the dawn wind was a strong easterly and too strong to push far off initially. The sea was carrying whitecaps, and it was quite cold as an early summer morning can so often be. I had a feeling though, that the wind would ease as the sun climbed higher in the sky. Mariners often say “The sun will burn off the wind!” We motored on to some shallow reef ground and contented ourselves with catching small black bream to 2lbs, small wrasse, dogfish, and a few mackerel for fresh baits. By 9.30am the wind had eased, the sea was flattening and it was much warmer with a patchy cloud sky. We took in the anchor and made our way, full speed, to the tope mark.

I was looking for a series of undulations that identified exactly where I wanted to be. The banks only rise off the seabed about 10 feet, with the tope running through the channels inbetween. I set the anchor making sure the boat was positioned so that our baits would fish directly in to the channel between the banks. We had four tope straight away, just as the tide was dropping towards low water. Over low water slack the bites fell away and I had to reposition the boat on the anchor and predict where I thought the channel would be once the tide flow increased enough to hold the boat steady on the anchor rope.

As the tide turned it took an hour for the boat to stop wandering on the rope and hold tight as the wind had picked up a little and was over riding the tide pull. We hit two more tope on Mike and Rob’s rods a little over an hour after low water. These were both fish about 30lbs. The runs started to come more quickly now, mostly pack tope between 22lbs and 30lbs, but Mike got a better fish about 35lbs. All these tope I was tagging too, so was ignoring my rod.

It was two hours after low water, always a great time for both numbers, and for big fish. I baited up with the head half of a fresh dab, my favourite tope bait. I dropped this over the side on a light lead and set the reel on a gentle ratchet so that line could pull off as a fish took the bait and ran.

The fresh bait had been on the seabed no longer than a couple of minutes when I had a pick up, then a slow steady run that did not seem to want to stop. I tend to hit tope early, usually just as they begin to slow down during the first run. This fish just kept going, so I waited a few more seconds, then clicked the reel back in to gear and let the rod bend to the fish. I felt a great weight and line started to pour off the reel, yet the tope was not running that fast. It kept running though, on and on and on, without stopping. The only thing to do was to keep the pressure on and try to turn the fish. It slowed, then went again, still not fast, but unstoppable.

While I was playing this fish, both Mike and Rob hooked up on other fish. Rob lost his when the hook just pulled out, then Mike fought his to the side of the boat and they landed it between them. Rob then hooked another, but eventually lost this one too, again when the hook just pulled free.

My fish was now well over 150 yards away, but had stopped running and was just using its weight to hang in the tide, shake its head, and twist its body. I started to pump the fish back towards me, inch by inch. It went on another long run, then turned and came back towards the boat, me winding like mad trying to keep a tight line. I kept the pressure on. It was getting closer, but remained a massive weight that now hugged the seabed and would not lift. The fish turned and took more line. It was now I said to Mike and Rob, this is a very big fish and we need to be quick when trying to land it. Mike had seen big tope landed before, but Rob was relatively new to tope fishing and had no experience of what to do. I tried to explain while still playing the fish.

The tope was now about 30 yards off the stern of the boat and still deep. I pressured the fish and slowly it came up. We saw a flash of white as it twisted in the tide, then a grey shape loomed up and the dorsal fin broke surface. The size, compared to tope I'd caught before, was huge. It had the length, but what shocked me was the barrel shaped belly giving the fish a massive girth. I played the fish to the side of the boat. The plan was that Mike, who was only 14-years-old or so, would grab the tail, Rob the dorsal fin, then hold the fish while I dropped the rod and grabbed the fish also by the tail and we'd lift it in over the low gunnel. Rob understandably, was hesitant and the first grab he missed. The second he grabbed the dorsal, but as the head of the tope turned round on him he let go, so did Mike. The fish put its head down and went back for the bottom on a searing run. I was expecting the line or tackle to part, but thankfully it held and I started to re play the fish all over again.

It was tired now and came back to the surface relatively easily. It wallowed on the surface, big and defiant. I inched it in to the gunnel. Mike grabbed the tail and this time, though still with some understandable hesitation, Rob grabbed the dorsal and held on. I was right between them and holding the tail we managed to lift the fish carefully aboard. It was huge. I measured the length and girth and applied the special formula that estimates the weight. It came out at about 85lbs. At the time it may have been a new UK boat record, but was certainly a new Welsh tope record, but after my regret with the record porbeagle, I had no intention of harming this fish. We took photos and I quickly tagged it. I could not lift the fish on my own for long, and then only to thigh height. Rob had to help me to lift the fish physically over the side. I held her in the water briefly to recover, and after less than a minute she was itching to swim away. I let my hands slip from under her and that great tail started to beat side to side, her head went down and she cruised effortlessly out of sight.

Over the coming years we took a lot of tope off those sandbanks. I had two more tope that measured out at 67lbs and 73lbs aboard *Lamna*, but never one quite as big as that initial monster.

Little did I know at the time, but this was not the last adventure with a big tope I was to have. I was about to come to grips with another, but this time off the shore.

ROCK LEDGE TOPE

I'd caught tope from the mid Wales surf beaches occasionally in the late 1980s, and on through the 1990s. Nothing huge, but nice fish to about 35lbs that fought like demons. To catch shore tope, conditions had to be just right. Warm, fairly settled weather, with a light onshore wind and calm sea ideally, but also a low tide falling early evening. If there was cloud cover, all the better. The tope used to then run the beaches, typically a little before dusk, and if the tide was just right, in to darkness as well right up to high water and maybe an hour after, then disappear. It was not easy fishing. When I thought conditions were perfect, the tope would often have other ideas. There was no real pattern to them moving tight inshore to feed. At best, it was 50/50 fishing.

I'd been fishing the rock ledges in North Wales pretty much every week with my fishing buddy Clive Griffiths around 2000. We'd had some great huss and conger fishing with fish to well over specimen size, but also done well on general species, including getting some ling to 5lbs, which of this size are not common off the shore locally, also specimen three-bearded rockling. We found that many of the usual marks were getting too popular with other anglers and were being fished too heavily resulting in dwindling catches. We began to explore the more remote areas with difficult and sometimes extreme access. This was to pay off big time!

We found one such rock ledge by accident. I was boat fishing one day when the skipper took us tight in looking for pollack. It's hard to be certain when looking shoreward as eyes can deceive, but I spied a ledge that looked like it was flat enough to allow two of us to fish it side by side, but with access to the water. Getting to it once on *terra firma* though, might prove difficult. A few weeks later, we went for a long walk taking no tackle. We followed a winding cliff path until we got to where I thought I'd seen the ledge. Access looked impossible from above. Being naturally inquisitive though, I always get down as close to the waters edge as I can when seeking out new marks, for sometimes, when walking cliff footpaths, you don't necessarily see ledges hidden by overhangs, or realise that what looks like vertical cliff, may actually be accessible. There was a sheer narrow gap in the cliffs, but there were good footholds, then a drop of about four feet on to a narrow ledge just wide enough for a man. This opened up then on to flattish rock and one of the easiest ledges we've ever fished from, and totally hidden from above. The sea level was about 15 feet below us, but there was access to the water down a rocky slope between rocks on to a finger of rock that was covered in barnacles, so this would give good grip. This rock finger would be prone to sea swells, but the access off, should the weather ever worsen, was good, and if this mark fished well, it would be an ideal spot for landing bigger fish.

The mark was not however, that easy to actually fish. Always in front of us, there were lobster and crab pots between 30 yards and 100 yards out, and to both left and right. By fishing the mark, we found that to the left was a sheer, deep underwater ledge that was just about impossible to drag fish of any size over. To the right a rocky reef disappeared underwater but extended out beyond us, and again it proved impossible to get the terminal tackle, and fish, back over it. The gap between the reef and ledge gave us a casting window of about 50 yards width about 50 yards out, just enough to fish two rods each. The depth though, dropped to 80 feet in places, and was still 40 feet right in front of us. It was pot luck where the crab pots would be laid by the potter, in addition to the length of rope used on the pots meant they would swing wildly either side of slack water. They were a nightmare to negotiate. After finding this mark, over the next few years we fished it a lot. Less in daylight, mostly at night. It fished well, producing a string of good conger, huss and ling, and also produced good numbers of smaller species too, such as rockling, codling, pollack, coalfish, big pouting, wrasse and even whiting at long range.

On the ledge one October night, I hit a fish that nearly pulled the rod clean out of the rest. It ran very fast for just a handful of seconds, then was gone. On retrieving the rig, the 100lb mono I'd been using as a conger trace was bitten clean through and the hook gone. I said to Clive I felt I'd just lost a tope. We fished on that night, but had no other indications that tope were, at that time, resident. We discussed what had happened in detail on the way home and wondered why we hadn't hit these fish before. It then dawned on me that the tope, this late in the year, were probably passing through heading back out to deeper water in the Irish Sea to over winter. They were there, but for how long? We put this in to practice, and that following November both lost big fish that ran. One lost quickly when the line abraded on rocks, the other getting the line tangled in a pot rope and breaking the line. We had no more encounters once December arrived. This gave us the inkling that the key time was the end of October to roughly the end of November. This would be the time we would concentrate on.

The 27th October 2001 saw low water fall at 23.30. The tide was a 27-footer and rising towards bigger spring tides. As we walked to the ledge, I glanced at my watch. It was 8.35pm. The sky was overcast with light cloud, just thin enough to let light filter through and we could just see without headlights the path in front of us. Headlights on now, we went down through the gap in the rocks, on to the narrow ledge, then on to the rock itself. The sea was calm, just a light swell creating white waves where it kissed the base of the rocks. A faint wind came in from the southwest, almost warm, but with a hint of damp about it too. The normal heavy mono traces were ignored. We tackled up with long pulley rigs that ended with 15 inches of 50lb multi-strand wire and a sharp 6/0 Viking 79515 pattern hook. We made long casts out in to the dark, heard the far off splash, allowed line to spill off the spool until we felt the bump as the lead weight hit the sea bed. Let the line sink, then slowly tighten the line until you just felt the lead weight. To move the weight might snag it.

An hour before low water I caught a 2lb pollack, then a small 8lb strap conger eel. Clive caught a poor cod, but smaller fish were surprisingly absent, which was unusual. We left the big baits down for up to 30 minutes, but they came back virtually untouched. Checking my watch it was getting near to low water. We both put fresh baits out, and settled back, the light from the lamp behind illuminating the reflective tape on our rod tips against the dark void in front of us. We both saw Clive's rod tip dip, bounce back, then heel over, butt lifting off the floor. He was on it in a flash, felt an almighty weight, the fish starting to rip line off the reel, then it was gone. He said, with a wry smile flickering across his face, "Certainly not a huss or conger!"

I re-baited choosing a third of a mackerel fillet cut towards the tail, then removed the head off a medium sized squid, cut through the body cavity lengthways, then wrapped this fully around the mackerel and bound it tight with elastic thread. It formed a neat sausage-shape on the hook and was oozing scent. I put a long

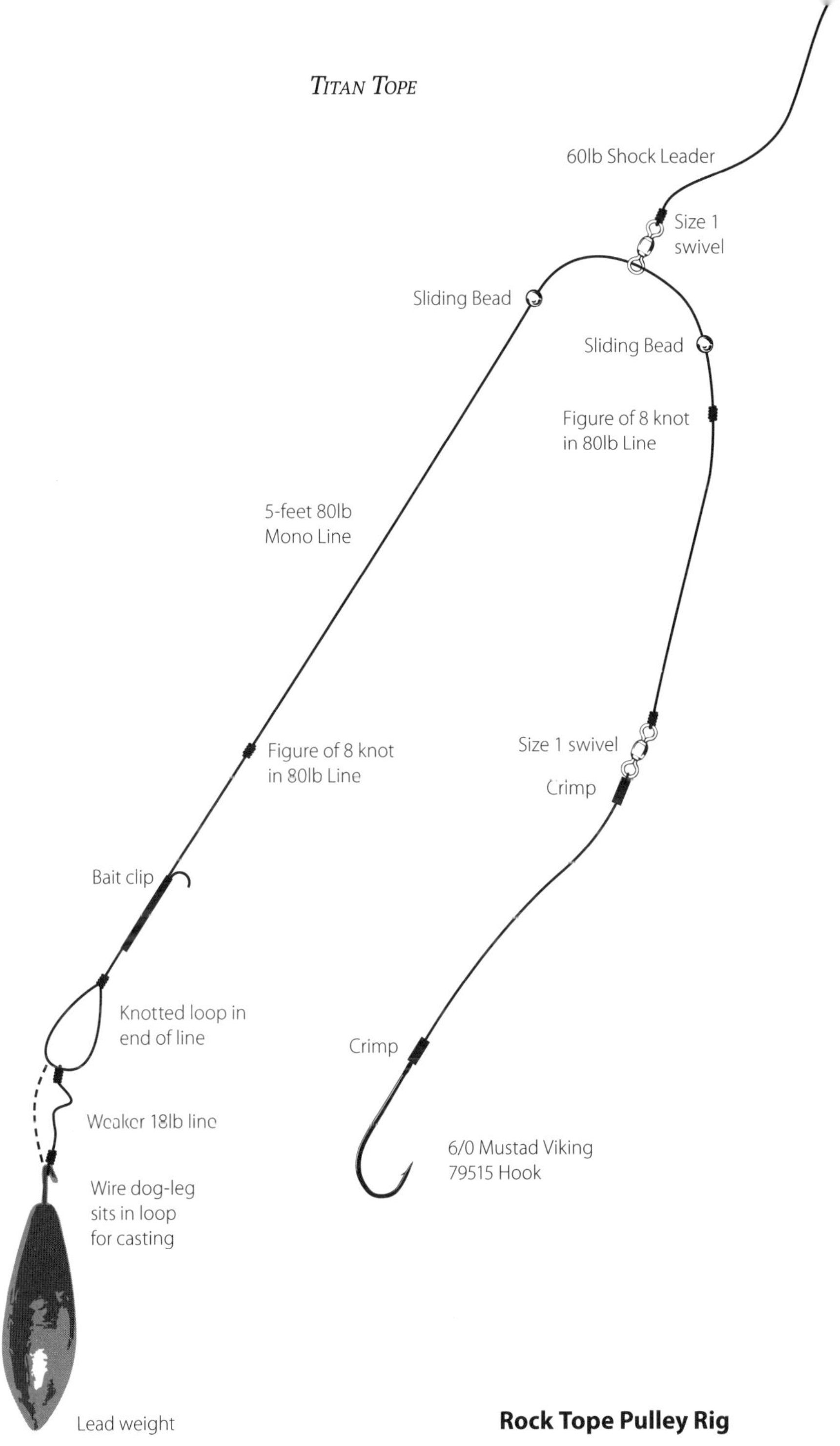

Rock Tope Pulley Rig

cast out in to what I knew was a slightly deeper gutter in amongst heavy rough ground and in about 70 feet of water. I glanced at my watch, the tide had just turned 10 minutes ago and we could hear the swell picking up slightly.

My reel was in free spool, but with the check on. I knew I could not let a big fish run, for the rough ground would soon break the line, but at the same time, I did not want a fish to feel the rod and the resistance of the line too much. I was looking at Clive, him chattering away, when the ratchet on my reel slowly clicked, then started to scream. I picked up the rod and the line was now flying off the spool. I let the fish run for just ten yards more, then put the reel in gear, clicked off the ratchet, and felt the rod buckle over to some enormous weight way out in the darkness. I felt a head shake, then line hissed off the reel, this causing little drops of mist like water the colour of rainbows that shot in to the air as my headlight beam passed through them. This fish was not for turning. It bored out and away from me at speed. It must have run for 30 yards or so, before rod pressure made it turn and it sped left, me trying to add a fraction of side strain to steer it away from a lobster pot that I knew was over on the left side. It thankfully turned again, going back to the right and taking more line off. Applying more side strain the fish still dragged more line off under heavy pressure, then went straight back out for the open sea. I was waiting for the horrible seesaw feel of my line on rope, but it didn't happen.

Suddenly the fish, still not really tiring, swam straight at me. I wound like fury trying to maintain a tight line, but I could not. I was waiting, heart in mouth, for that realisation that the hook had pulled free, or the line parted, but as I kept winding the line tightened and I felt the surge of the fish, now only 40 yards or so out, but deep down. The real weight of the fish came to bear now, the line almost vertical in the water and the rod tip pulled hard over and pulsing to the swimming fish, as it twisted and turned, thrashing its tail. I was sweating heavily, but could only work the fish as hard as I could trying to gain precious line and get the fish up in the water column away from the many snags. It hung deep. I felt the fish pause, maybe thinking what to do next, then it turned to the right and swam fast for the reef. Heavy side strain just managed to turn it and I felt it wallow down deep and out of sight.

Clive knew what to do and needed no prompting. He made his way down to the rocky finger, now splashed by the rising swell. I worked the massive weight upwards, bit by bit, the fish coming grudgingly, then taking a few feet of line back, this occurring for maybe a couple of minutes or more. My eyes strained through the dark following my powerful headlight beam, trying to see what was down there. The fish was close now. Clive shouted he could see the top of my shock leader. I saw a huge white shape roll just under the surface and a massive shark-like tail smack the water and dive down a dozen feet or more. I could feel now, the fish was tired and about to give in. It showed on the surface again and just wallowed there. I worked the fish back towards Clive by walking the edge of the ledge above, but towards him. There was a little gap between the rock finger where Clive was below, and the cliff edge I was standing on. I steered the nose of the fish through the gap and Clive shouted, clearly and well above the murmur of the swell breaking on the rocks, "A tope! Its bloody huge!" Holding the fish on the heavy trace, he manoeuvred it in to the edge and grabbed the wrist of the tail, but could not lift the fish on to the rock. Looking at the fish by the side of Clive, I knew from its length and heavy gut it was a 50lber.

I grabbed the camera and went down on to the rocky finger. Together we gently lifted the fish up on to a safe clean bed of rock, but I slipped and in putting my hand out to save myself slid my hand across sharp barnacles. I straddled the fish on my knees to make sure she did not hurt herself when struggling. We tried to length and girth the tope using some mono shock leader, and based on a mathematical formula she came out at later at well over 50lbs. I tried to lift the tope for a photo, but she was too heavy for a clean lift and I needed Clive to help put her on to my knees. I noticed her lower body had blood on it, but it was mine. I saw a deep gash on my palm, caused by contact with the barnacles, was dripping blood at an alarming rate, yet the adrenalin coursing through me meant I felt no pain. We got the photos, but I wanted this fish back in the water. Me cradling the fish by the head and upper body, Clive supporting the tail and body, we shuffled to the water's edge, lowered her in to position and slid her in to the water. We watched, still starstruck by the sheer size of the fish, as she stirred back to life. She tried to move her tail, but I held her for a little longer, then felt strength return to her. At the next kick of the tail I reluctantly let go. With short but powerful side-to-side tail movements she dropped her nose and swam for the depths. We watched as the clear shape of the fish changed to a fuzzy grey and white, watched the white fade to a blur, then fade to nothing...and the fish was gone.

We sat on the top of the ledge for five minutes, talking about what we'd just witnessed, both almost wondering if what we'd seen was real, and that it had actually happened. We knew it had, yet it felt surreal. We were covered in slime, me in blood, and the photos were secure in the camera, if we needed proof. How big was she? When young, I could lift 55lb bags of cement, but not easily, and when I tried to lift this tope, she felt the same. We've had other tope since from the ledge, but never anywhere near as big, though we have both lost big fish after a few minutes' fight, either the ropes, the reef, or the ledge being the tope's ally. The hard fought battle, the shock at the size of the fish on the rock, and the release are all etched clearly in my mind. Sometimes, when my mind is idle and far away, I may glance at my right hand, see the line of a faint scar on the palm, and relive one of the highlights of my angling life.

Chapter 7
The Numbers Game

As my fishing interests developed in the late 1980s, and took various new avenues, I started to take note of how many species I'd caught each year. This was, on average, some 25 or so different fish over the calendar year. I wasn't, at the time, targeting all these fish, these were just what I naturally caught when fishing for other species.

I'd also realised early on that competitive match fishing was just not for me. I did dabble with it briefly, and did okay, at least at local club level. Its not that I don't admire match anglers. I do, and very much so! There is great skill in constantly being in the placings, but in my opinion, it does not cover enough variety, so did not appeal to me personally. I'd also covered quite a few matches for angling magazines during the 80s, and the so-called camaraderie and brotherhood you often read about amongst match anglers was just not always what it should be. I witnessed some poor behaviour, to say the least. Besides I wanted to experience a wider range of sea fishing, not concentrate on just one aspect, as I'd done when solely targeting bass. I did realise though, that I still needed a competitive edge to my fishing. Something to motivate me, get me thinking, and trying new things. It struck me a good way to start would be to target a certain number of species each year.

I set about putting together a set of ground rules. My year would be, obviously, 1st of January to the 31st of December. I would include sea fish caught from both boat and shore. I also wanted a definitive geographical boundary to fish within from the outset. I realised that the boundary had to be financially realistic regards travel, but with multiple challenges within that area. I briefly thought about restricting myself to just the coastline of Wales, but then thought this too restrictive as I was travelling all over the UK fairly regularly to work, and each year to Ireland. I decided to include species caught within UK and Irish waters.

The other rules were that my fish would be obviously rod and line caught, and that any fish species would count, big or small. I decided to not allow myself any foul-hooked fish. In competitive match fishing, some rules allow the landing of foul-hooked fish, if the hook is in the vicinity of the mouth. My thoughts on this were that maybe the fish did attack the bait and simply miss it, much like a bird of prey can, but the fish was not correctly hooked and therefore could not be classed as a genuine catch. My decision was that for any fish to count in my species list, it had to be hooked fair and square inside the mouth. The only other original rule I had was that for a fish to count as caught, either I, a companion, or a boat skipper, had to touch the leader or hook snood leading directly to the hook, or alternatively I touched the fish during unhooking and release. Touching the leader with the fish at the boat side is classed as a 'catch' as it allows the fish to be released in the water without needing to be landed.

These then were my basic guidelines. Necessary rules to self-police my fishing and keep me totally honest. There would be no point doing this if things were not completely true and forever consistent. I also figured that if need be, should a circumstance arise, that I could add a rule at a later date to cover a specific eventuality.

I remember I started by making a list of the fish, that in my home waters, were supposedly easy to catch. This was, again on average, some 22 locally common species. This tallied up with my average annual count of about 25. This suggested my initial annual target should be 30. I compiled a list of an additional ten species I wasn't catching in the course of my local fishing, and started, much as I did with the bass in the early days, to research them. For example, spotted ray are only normally caught on two shore venues in my immediate local waters, and I wasn't fishing either of them at the time. Using past catch reports, word of mouth, and general research, I learnt the best time, tides and baits for spotted ray and over a three year period gathered enough information to be able to pretty much guarantee myself one or more every season. I'd caught garfish plenty of times previously, but usually by accident when spinning for mackerel and school bass. I knew where and when to go for them, I just needed to switch to a more conventional means of fishing for them to make them a relatively easy catch. Getting to 30 species was not actually that difficult, but it was a number that showed willing. The true enormity of what you're trying to achieve is when you raise the bar to 40 species within the calendar year.

This was where boat fishing came in, and those occasional trips further afield, but especially my trips to Ireland. I had to learn quickly. On the boat you would see an angler pulling haddock out while you were hitting only whiting. You would notice that tub gurnard required a different approach than grey and red gurnard do. Also realising the moment that there were pilchard in amongst the mackerel and having the forethought to duly drop down to small fish skin feathers on tiny size 10 hooks to pick them up, and so on and so on. It was all so often about having the right rigs ready at a moments notice. Also being able to adapt and ring the changes according to the species in front of you. I watched my boat tackle box expand rapidly regards the amount of tackle it contained as I tried to cover all eventualities.

Its important to remember that I was not fishing more and more frequently to catch an increased number of species. My diary tells me that I was fishing about the same overall number of trips each year, this governed by what free time I had available. Just like everyone else I had to work full time, and being a freelance journalist meant I had to create my own work each and every week, so fishing time was not easy to come by. What was making the difference was my willingness to adapt, make mistakes, learn from them, and slowly formulate the knowledge in my head to enable me to target a species with real intent.

Looking back at my diary entries I climbed steadily from the 30 species, to the low 30s, then the high 30s by the end of 1990s. This was a progressive learning curve with no quick fix. I finally broke 40 species for the first time in 2001. The next obvious target was to try for 50, but having achieved 40 in 12 months, and understanding how hard it is to get to 40 species in a single year, 50 seemed a near impossible goal. It was back to the drawing board to compile a list of species again, that I rarely caught. Then research them fully, and try to organise specific trips where I was in with a chance of catching them.

Originally I'd intended to target the mini species more, such as goldsinny wrasse, corking wrasse, the gobies, sea scorpions, shannies and others. I did catch a few of these during normal fishing, and I had the occasional specific trip for them as early as the late 1980s, but now started to target them deliberately. This was a relatively quick fix and ensured me at least another six or seven species a year. My annual tally climbed and I did 45 in 2004, and 47 in 2005, then dropped back to 38 in 2006 and 37 in 2007. The reason for the drop back in numbers were both years saw poor weather, pretty much throughout, and boat trips were at a minimum. Also my work load was such that I had to cut back on the number of overall trips I made. However the results from 2004 and 2005 gave me encouragement that I was knocking on the right door.

2008 was again blighted by weather, the Meteorological Office confirming it was the coldest year for over 30 years, often wet and windy, and with a cold winter. I was also working away from home for a lot of the time too, so I only got to 33 species. The weather was poor again in 2009, but I raised my game and got 41 species. It was hard fishing though, and I knew in my own heart I'd made the best of the opportunities I had that year.

I wasn't too disheartened after the four relatively poor years. The diary, as ever, kept me logical suggesting why things had not gone according to plan. As 2010 came in, I had a reasonable start and was on 17 species by late April. But by early August, just prior to leaving for a trip to Ireland, I was only on 24. Travelling over on the ferry I was thinking that, with luck, I might get to 40 by the end of the year, if I fished well in Ireland. The Emerald Isle has always been a lucky country for me, and this time she was even more generous. When I came home, I was on 42 species. I still thought 50 was out of reach!

In the first two weeks of September, two deliberate trips to Anglesey's north coast to target mini species added sand goby, black goby, long spined sea scorpion, leopard spotted goby, sand smelt, goldsinny wrasse and tompot blenny. I was fishing the last trip with a friend, Colin Albert from Cardiff, another species hunter. He was excited I was on 49. We were fishing the breakwater at Holyhead, and I said to him, I've got a chance of a shore rockling from a small piece of ground by the breakwater wall where I've had them before. I dropped a two-hook rig with size 6 hooks on baited with small slivers of mackerel ... and second cast I got my shore rockling. I'd done it, caught 50 sea species within the calendar year! I boat fished off Eastbourne the 22nd of September and added a black bream, went to Plymouth and bagged a thornback ray, which surprisingly I'd missed out on all year, and finished back on my own turf fishing a rock ledge on the 1st of December bagging a three-bearded rockling. 53 species for the year!

Looking back now, and understanding how much fishing effort and research I had to put in to get those 53 species, I feel those who feel the urge to follow, that 50 is the Holy Grail. It's a huge number of species, many requiring specific tackle and techniques to catch them, as well as a detailed understanding of the ground over which they can be found. I've since heard that other anglers have exceeded this total, and if done genuinely, then I can only tip my hat to you. To do 50, or more, within the year, then you need to not just work hard, but also have major chunks of luck, and a massive amount of free time. That year I didn't get a chance to fish for smoothound at all, there was no time for a mullet trip, I missed out on a small-eyed ray, and I didn't get a greater weever, all fish that I would normally expect to catch in an average year. You will have failures, it is inevitable. It will never all go right for you. Could I have done better? Frankly, no! Looking back, other than swap work time for more fishing time, which was not practical and would have been downright irresponsible, I could not have done more that year. It was a coming together of a huge amount of hard work and effort over more than 20 years to learn as much as I could about each different species that brought me to that point. Would I do it again? Yes, and I hope too at some stage. But as we'll now see, things moved on again to another level!

A TOTAL SPECIES COUNT

Inevitably, while trying hard to climb the total species in a year table, it quickly dawned on me that it might be interesting to tot up my total species count within UK and Irish waters. I hadn't done this prior to 1990 and found I was on 43 sea species. I'd also done a little freshwater fishing over the years, so decided to run both salt and freshwater fish together to form one all-time caught list within the UK and Ireland. This, at the time, got me to just 52 species in total. This presented another challenge. Could I target 100 species caught in UK and Irish waters in my lifetime? Looking at the 52 I'd already got, these being pretty much the easiest to be caught given my home location, then it looked, and was, a big ask, but one I felt worth bearing in mind.

Although I would apply the same logic I use when targeting any fish to this quest, I decided on a slightly different approach. This time I chose to target small groups of fish by their likelihood of being caught. Should a trip be possible to a new venue, I would pick out a possible species resident there I had not yet caught, and go principally for that. This is easier said than done when those around you are hauling out quality turbot and plaice, and you are trying everything you know to hook a brill, but failing. It takes a strong will to stay on course.

I had caught a couple of difficult species within that initial 52 species, principally a 42lb monkfish which, if I'd not already got this on my list, come the future, it would have been one that would have been exceptionally difficult to catch due to commercial over fishing severely depleting their numbers. The mission to catch as many species in the year was obviously my biggest advantage. Targeting these inevitably brought in to play some species I had not caught before, so I started to quite quickly add new species initially, and then right through the 1990s. Then, as we entered the new millennium, things naturally started to slow down. By then I'd caught around 85 species, and it was obviously getting ever harder with each one added. In 2004 I caught just one new fish, my one and only john dory while fishing the Magharees Reef in Tralee Bay, County Kerry. 2005 was better and I added another four. In 2006 I again added just one, a common goby. Only a bleak came my way in 2007, and 2008 saw me add two more including a zander. I was on 94 species in total now, but wondering where the next one would come from.

The weather, and the fishing, in 2009 was generally very poor, but I added a tommy ruffe, and a three-spined stickleback. I'd also known for some time there were golden-grey mullet to be caught at Llangennith Beach in South Wales, but never yet had time to go and try for them. However I went down and fished with Colin Albert on the 8th of September, specifically for them, and caught six golden-greys to 2lb 1oz on maddie rag baits. I was now on 97.

Working as an angling writer, through my work, I was to meet and work alongside Mike Hennessy. Mike was a Fisheries Information Officer with Inland Fisheries Ireland. He proved to be a serious angling addict the same as me. His interest and forte was in catching species and specimen fish. I doubt any two anglers could have been in tune better than Mike and I were. Although my job when over there was to get magazine features, and work always did come first on these trips as the resulting features proved, but when possible we would fish the clock round and try to catch both specimens and new species for me.

In August 2010, the year I got the 53 species in the year, I started up in Donegal, and made my way down to County Kerry.

Mike's 42lb boat caught Monkfish (1986)

I needed a triggerfish, and one of Mike's contacts, Kevin Brain, a tackle dealer and fishing guide from Waterville, also knew and said he would bear it in mind when fishing with clients. Mike and I were fishing for wrasse, when the phone rang. It was Kev, "Get yourselves over here, there are triggerfish all over the place". Never have you seen two anglers pack gear up so quickly and hammer off down the road to the triggerfish venue. Walking, or was it flat out running, I seem to remember the latter, we arrived on a steep rock ledge. Kev then said, "Sorry guys, they seem to have disappeared". Typical, always the same scenario. I felt that all too familiar pill of disappointment appear in my stomach. We decided to add some small fist sized balls of mashed up bran, oil and mackerel in to the water, and by luck, out of the depths, loomed a large shoal of triggerfish. I couldn't believe my eyes! I'd rigged float gear and was watching the float intensely. It did not move even though there were triggers a few feet under the bait. Mike caught two triggers straight away, and somehow I managed to hook a 6lb conger. Yes, on float gear. What was I doing wrong?

The sea was calm with no swell, the float inert and just sitting there. I quickly found that by casting out slightly beyond the triggers, then pulling the float in over the top of them, then letting the bait fall naturally in the water, they would lift up and grab it. Success! I caught six to 2lbs 3ozs on small mackerel strip baits in quick succession before they lost interest and disappeared. Number 98!

We were scheduled to fish out from Cahersiveen on the 27th August. If the weather held and conditions were calm, the intention was to travel out to what is called the ten-mile reef. This is a deep water mark and is where the seabed starts to initially shelve off towards the deeper water of the continental shelf. I was told there was a very good chance of catching a bluemouth, a member of the Redfish family, and a species that was new to me.

The day dawned warm and sunny, with a light northwest wind. The sea though, was choppy with a good swell. Heading out to the reef dolphin broached either side of the boat, some coming in to play and ride the bow wash as they often do. We also saw big fish scatter the surface in the distance. These were probably albacore, as there were a lot in this area at the time. Arriving over the reef the skipper judged the tide and wind, and set us up on a drift up one side of the reef, over the top, and down the other. The peak of the reef was about 400 feet depth dropping away either side in to much deeper water. I was fishing luminous tube lures on smaller size 2/0 hooks baited with mackerel strip to deliberately target the bluemouth. Mike and another angler onboard caught blue mouth straight away. All I could seem to catch were ling, pollack and coalfish during the first two drifts.

The third drift I changed over to a heavier weight, this to allow me to 'feel' the weight just bouncing the reef as the boat drifted over it. This worked. I got hit by a double thump and felt weight on the rod tip. Whatever was down there was heavy and fighting using head shakes. I slowly gained line, bringing the fish ever higher. It was a triple header. A ling on the bottom hook, coalfish on the top hook, and sat proudly in the middle was my first ever bluemouth. A stunning orange coloured fish with a defiantly high, sharp spined dorsal fin and big beautiful eyes indicative of a fish that lives at depth. I caught maybe 40 of them that day. Number 99! Oh, so close now!

Returning home from Ireland, and still trying for my 50 species that year remember, I went up to the North Wales coast. I'd found out that a few leopard spotted gobies were caught from a couple of the small piers and breakwaters there. I could kill two birds with one stone here, gaining another species for the year, and also catch a new species for my all time list. The fishing was simple. I used a light one-hook rig with the short six-inch hook link tight behind the lead weight and ending in a size 12 hook. I baited with small chunks of ragworm, and after a succession of small wrasse, shannies and black gobies, I got my leopard spotted goby. In fact five of them. Colin Albert was with me, and I did a little jig of delight on the pier end, then we celebrated with a hot cup of coffee made on Col's little stove. Number 100!

It didn't really hit me until I was home, sat on my own with a bottle of beer. I got to thinking back to when I was on a total of 52, and it seemed such a long time ago. At that time 100 seemed impossible, yet I'd finally achieved it. I was elated, yet at the same time, felt a little subdued, for once a long term ambition is achieved, a life purpose is taken away.

I wondered, very briefly, whether to continue targeting new species after this, but quickly realised that if I were to stop, I would miss the chase. Besides it had become such a big part of my fishing life, and I enjoyed the challenge, the research, and even the disappointments. At the time of writing, summer 2015, I'm now on 110 species. Averaging two a year since getting over 100 has been a surprise. The intention now is just to keep chipping away and add as many as I can. I have 120 in mind, but would be happy with 115 realistically.

Before I end on species, its fair to warn you that once bitten, it is infectious. It can take over your whole fishing life. As well as my yearly and total lists, I also run lists on all the shore fish I've caught in Wales, a total species caught in Wales list, and the same for Ireland, also species I've caught on the fly. I also compiled a list of the fish I've caught in the Eastern Atlantic, that is Europe, Scandinavia and Iceland, which now totals some 128 different fish. That decision I took to target species way back in 1980s has given me a lifetime of fishing fun, as well as a life purpose, and kept me competitive within myself.

In the next chapter, we'll move on to my pursuit of specimen fish, and why I find this form of fishing equally as challenging.

Chapter 8
In Pursuit Of Specimen Fish

Every angler wants to catch at least some big fish. If you fish often enough, the law of averages will see you triumph, at least some of the time. But what if you want to catch big fish on a regular basis, and almost to order? Then it becomes much more difficult, and the amount of effort you need to put in to be successful climbs proportionately. It takes a single-minded dedication to be a specimen hunter.

Another trap set to catch me was the pursuit of specimen fish. I'm not sure when I became a specimen hunter. It was born in me when I started targeting those big bass back in the 80s maybe. As I targeted different species for my species lists, again it was an already smouldering natural progression that would lead me in to regularly seeking out the bigger fish. Living where I did in North Wales, the specimen weights compiled by the Welsh Federation of Sea Anglers made the best starting point.

The first question to ask though, is exactly what is a specimen fish? Giving this some thought at the time, and working with specimen fish lists from several quarters, including the WFSA, I decided that a specimen fish, in the majority of cases, should be a fish that weighs at least 70% of the national record. With further consideration though, this does not always work out. Look at bass for instance. The record is now close to 20lbs, but the reality is that very few bass over 10lbs in weight, by number, are caught. 10lbs has been the specimen weight for bass for as long as I can remember. It remains a valid ceiling to achieve today, due to the overall low numbers of fish of this size being caught. Shore conger eel would be another. The shore conger record has broken 70lbs, yet the chance of a 50lb-plus conger off the shore, simply due to the sheer size and difficult terrain these big eels are found in, is maybe a step too far. In the case of conger eels, then a 40lb fish would be the logical weight a shore caught eel would need to achieve to be classed as a true specimen. Blue shark fell in to the same category. It was hard to get a blue over 100lbs during the 80s, 90s and virtually right through until the late 2000s. The heavy predation by man at sea on sharks for the commercial value of their fins had a massive effect on the size of blue shark available off the UK coast. Although the record was then just over 200lbs, it had stood since the late 1950s. You could not justifiably target a 150lb blue as a specimen as the chances of catching one were very limited. A target of 100lbs was much more sensible, at the time.

It was obvious that, preferring to fish outside any club or organisation, my specimen list needed to be a personal one that suited my own fishing, and took in to consideration local limitations on certain species. For the first years I used the 70% marker as my main target weight, but would reluctantly adjust a weight for a specific fish if I knew that a factor of 70% would be almost impossible to achieve.

One of my first targeted fish to try and catch a specimen was a thornback ray, and this was even before I went species hunting. Thornbacks were, at the time, very common within my home waters of Cardigan Bay. I'd set my target at 12lbs off the shore. Rays up to 8lbs were fairly regularly caught, but fish over a genuine 10lbs off the shore were not. I was fishing the surf beaches a fair bit for the rays in the late 80s, and I'd noticed two periods when there was a chance of a bigger than average fish. One was in mid May to late June, but that was dependent if the weather was calm over the bigger spring tides. The best time was very late in the year, from mid October through to early November. If there was a short spell of gales or stormy weather during this short window, and again if it coincided with the bigger spring tides, then as the sea settled but remained coloured, a night tide could produce some good catches of rays.

It was the 29th of November, 1988. The previous three days had seen a gale blow in from the west with winds swinging from the northwest to the southwest. The tide was 30-foot, and just dropping away after the biggest tides of that cycle. High water was at 22.15. The wind was light from the east, and big stars shimmered and flashed in what was an otherwise oily black sky. Fishing the hour and a half up to high water I had a succession of dogfish. High tide came and went. Now the tide was ebbing I put more power in to my casts and was putting smallish mackerel baits out a very long way, this aided by fishing just 12lb main reel line on my multiplier reel to minimise air drag and towed weight during the cast. Some 20 minutes after high water, I saw the rod tip nod three times, straighten, then pull over as a fish pulled out the grip lead. Feeling the fish way out in the tide, it felt heavy, and made short runs when tight in to the surf. It was a thornback ray weighing a little over 5lbs. Next cast I got another of 7lbs, followed by a ray only slightly smaller. Two casts later, the bait had been out no more than five minutes when the rod tip just pulled hard over, pulsed a few times, then as I picked up the rod I noticed that the line was falling slack. Winding in fast I felt the weight of the fish, and this was no ordinary ray. Its weight buckled the rod over and I could feel the fish settle on the seabed, and suction down with its wings. A minute or so of steady pressure moved the fish. It swam in to a deeper gully running parallel with the shore and took a few yards of line. I played the fish way out in the deeper gutter for a short while, then applied more pressure and forced it out of the gully on to shallower sand. It came through the surf trying to run parallel away from me and to the right. It turned and I saw it wing tips clear of the surface in my headlight. I waited for a short wave, then let this wash the fish ashore by walking it back on a tight line. This was a big ray. My friend Clive Griffiths lifted the fish up by the wing edges and it looked massive. It later weighed 12lb 3ozs. A thick, heavily set fish with a deep body. In my home waters, off the shore, it was a specimen. I'll never better this fish, or at least I'm unlikely to do so now, for a short time after this, the commercial tangle netters decimated the rays within Cardigan Bay, and to this day, their numbers remain a shadow of what they once where.

13lb shore caught Cod - Cardigan Bay

My next target was a cod over 10lbs from my local area. Cod are not a common catch within Cardigan Bay. Those that are caught are usually under 5lbs, but with the odd bigger fish to 8lbs, if you know where to go. I'd been catching cod consistently over a few winters and found that the best chance of a bigger fish was when the smaller codling started to thin out just after Christmas. I was watching the weather patterns for a period of gales, then would head out and fish a big spring tide, with a big sea running, to try my luck. This turned out to be the 10th of January, 1989. It was a 30.3-foot tide, the biggest tide of the cycle. High water was at 22.20, low water falling about 04.45. The southwest wind was force 4 and building, with gusts to force 6 and sometimes 7. The sea was heavy and crashing, created by the recent gales and encouraged again by the steadily increasing wind. There was weed in the water on my first casts. A little after high water I saw the rod bounce. Not sure if it was weed, I waited and it knocked again. I struck and felt a satisfying weight with some shaking of the head. It was a codling close to 3lbs, and a welcome sign that I was not all mad to be out in this foul and worsening weather.

I had nothing then for the next four hours. Dispirited I poured a coffee from my flask and huddled up under the sea wall for some slight respite from the now dreadful wind and persistent driving rain. While drinking, and wondering if it was time to pack up encouraged by the thought of a warm bed, I noticed that a short distance down the beach, beyond the gap between two groynes, the surf was shorter and breaking a little closer in. To both left and right of this, the surf was breaking further out. This indicated deeper water, either a washed-out bowl, or section of beach where a short gully had dug out. I moved down, but trying to get the first cast away, the surge of the waves being high, it meant I had to half-run down as one wave ebbed away, make a quick cast, then rush back before the next waist high surge caught up with me.

Making my second cast, there was just enough time to get a really good pendulum cast away. The big lug bait sailed out a fair way, before the wind and line drag took the speed out of the lead weight. Holding the rod high I walked back and decided to hold the rod vertical to minimise the chance of weed snagging the line close in. I was starting to dream about that warm bed, when I felt just a single knock on the rod tip. As I decided whether it was just weed, the rod tip hammered right over, the weight broke free, and a heavy weight bounced the rod. I instantly knew this was a cod as it shook its head violently, then turned and slowly dragged line from the reel as it fought somewhere far out in the hostile blackness. The fish felt heavy, stubborn, and reluctant to come in towards me. It made two runs, dragging maybe ten yards of line off, then rested as I pumped it closer to shore. As it felt the surf shallowing, it was off again, first to the left taking line, then to the right running parallel with the shore and away from me. I followed it, held the rod high, and waited for each wave to lift the weight of the fish, then retrieved line as it washed the beast closer to shore. The fish, right at the edge of the wave now, made one last outward dash, but it was tiring and I steered its head back towards me as a wave splashed ashore. I saw the fish right at the edge of the water, its tail slapped up and down lazily. I ran down the beach a few yards, the fish's head still facing towards me. Only as I got to the fish did I see the size and length of it. It was a prime cod, fat in the belly, with a solid head and mottled fawny brown flanks. I buried my hand deep in its gill and lifted the fish. It was heavy, very heavy. As I walked back to dry sand, even in the pitch darkness, heavy rain, and it being the early hours of the morning, I glanced up and down the beach to see if anyone had seen me land the fish. I was alone, sole witness to what I had in my hand. A prize taken from a wild storm beach on a night sane people were safe in their homes. Later that morning I weighed the fish at exactly 13lbs. Not big by some standards and for some regions, but for my coast, where cod are scarce, a veritable monster.

Over the next few years I spent more time targeting specimen fish. These included big flounder, huss, dab, three bearded rockling, tope and black bream. All fish over a true specimen weight, and all deliberately targeted. It was during my visits to Ireland though, and when fishing with Norman Dunlop, who was the full-time Sea Angling Advisor to the Fisheries Board, that I became aware of the Irish Specimen Fish Committee specimen list. This was a revelation. It was impeccably run with a totally strict protocol to be followed when claiming a fish, a logical and high weight to be achieved for each species, and what's more it was national throughout Ireland, but also open to anyone fishing in the beautiful Emerald Isle.

When you're fishing as I was, mainly for angling magazine features, and consequently spending much of the time with a camera in hand rather than a fishing rod, it was impractical to deliberately target specific species as specimens. It was a case of getting a little fishing time in as and when action on the boat had diminished, or when I had the full compliment of photos I needed and was then only looking for something special to really enhance a feature. However, what the camera did, was give me the opportunity to observe what other anglers were doing, identify what was down there, then when I did get a chance to fish myself, make the very most of it.

I didn't start targeting Irish specimen fish until 2004, quite late considering my quest for big fish in Welsh waters. I did though, miss out on a few through the late 1990s. I lost out on a coalfish that looked close to 15lbs that I caught on a wreck off Culdaff. This fish was kept for weighing ashore, and was on top of a small box of edible fish the skipper wanted to retain for eating. I briefly left the boat to take a photograph of the harbour for the feature, and when I returned the fish box had gone. I was also with Paul Harris, then an Angling Tourism officer with Tourism Ireland, and caught a 5lb 1oz ballan wrasse. We were in a very isolated area, far away from shops with accredited scales, and I had no wish to kill the fish, so returned it immediately. I had pollack over Irish specimen weight, also grey mullet, but was not, at that time, in a position to get them weighed, and would have returned the mullet alive anyway.

From 2000 onwards the Irish Specimen scene seemed to suddenly grow at a rapidly quickening pace with more and more anglers becoming involved. This led to an increasing number of anglers, and skippers, carrying accredited scales, or having access to accredited scales via shops. This making it easier to get fish officially weighed and confirmed.

It was in 2004 that I made a conscious effort to target the Irish Specimen Fish Committee's 10 Specimens award. This signifies that you have caught ten specimen-sized fish. These can be all different species, or have the same species several times. My intention was just to target what presented itself, and to maximise any opportunity.

On the 7th September, 2004, I was fishing with skipper Danny MaCarthy off Brandon Head in County Kerry. With me were Norman Dunlop and my son Mike Jr. We started hitting big spurdog, and I realised there was the chance of getting a 12lb-plus fish, a specimen. We all fished hard, and I thought I'd done it when I caught a big spur, but it weighed 2ozs short of the required weight.

The following day, the 8th, the wind had shifted from the southwest to the northwest and it was fresh. The drift off Brandon Head was too fast to fish, so Danny decided to anchor up. The ground here is broken sand and rock and is alive with red, grey and tub gurnards, along with haddock, cod, ling, huss, pollack and much more. At anchor, the ground we were fishing on was fairly hard rock with just the odd patch of sand. Norman mentioned that there was a really good chance of a very big tub gurnard from this area. This was my trigger and I set about to catch one. I knew from targeting the gurnards when counting species that tub gurnard are especially attracted to the colour pink. I set up a two-hook trace with small three-inch pink muppets above the hook, which was baited with fresh mackerel strip. I'd also learnt that gurnards, as are many other fish, are attracted to sound, especially rhythmic monotonous sound. I fished by adjusting the lead weight so that it was just heavy enough to keep me in constant contact with the seabed, then continually lifted and dropped it so that the weight was banging on the rock below giving out a constant "tap tap tap". I'd been catching a host of species including red and grey gurnard, haddock, codling, ling to 10lbs, pollack and coalfish. Then I got a single, sudden, savage hit. On striking the fish, it fought doggedly, head down and reluctant to leave the seabed. It fought using a series of triple knocks as it came up through the water column. I saw the reddy orange of a big tub gurnard in the gin clear water when it was still maybe 20 feet down. It looked big, and proved to be a specimen and weighed 5lb 13ozs. I decided to continue fishing the same way to see if there was another big tub down there. About an hour later, I hit another good fish, and from the fight felt straight away it was a big tub. This fought longer and much harder, and as the fish broke surface there was huge shout from Norman, who said, "Its huge, much bigger than the last". He was right too. It weighed 8lbs 13ozs! Two Irish specimens in a day!

One of the most difficult specimens to get is a garfish. For some reason a just sub-2lb garfish is not overly hard to catch, but then adding another three ounces or so to get over the specimen weight, set then at 2lbs 2ozs, was very hard. I was off Ballycotton Island in East Cork fishing with Peter Manning aboard his boat *Cleona*. Norman was with me and I'd had blue shark the previous day, but we wanted to try the ground fishing and enjoyed some great sport with cod to 12lbs, good ling and general ground species such as whiting, gurnards, haddock and pollack. We also had a bag of mashed mackerel and bran out looking to see if we could interest another shark. This pulled in a lot of garfish which worked inside the oil slick made by the rubby dubby. Both Norman and I set up spinning rods with just a small swivel tied to the end of the line, then six-feet of 12lb Fluorocarbon and tied on a size six hook. We cut small, thin strips from the belly section of a fresh mackerel, and nicked these to the hook just by passing the hook point in through one end only. This I free-lined back in to the dubby slick letting just the weight of the swivel slowly drop the bait deeper.

It was a rough sea pushed up by a strong southwest wind. The bites from the garfish were sudden. They would take, then dash sideways, and almost immediately come up from maybe ten feet down and leap clear of the water, or porpoise in and out across the surface. We had a lot of gars that day. In excess of 20 each, the majority between 1lb and 1.5lbs in weight. But we also had two or three fish that nudged the 2lb mark, and these seemed to be working deeper than the smaller ones. I pinched on a small BB split shot about two feet above the hook and fed this down through the water. I caught two good gars close to 2lbs in quick succession. Then nothing. I kept plugging away, then got a savage tug and struck. This gar came clean out of the water vertically, tail thrashing thin air. It was maybe 20 feet away from me, and it looked big. It fought all the way to the boat on the light tackle, and Peter had to net it. Back ashore it weighed 2lbs 3ozs on accredited scales and was another specimen.

I had to wait until 2010 before I got the chance to add another Irish specimen, then got two in one day. These being off Cahersiveen and were a Bluemouth of 2lbs 4ozs, just 2ozs under the then Irish record, also a cuckoo wrasse of 1lb 6ozs. In July of 2012, I was fishing with skipper Kit Dunne aboard the *Lisen 2* off Wicklow, Ireland. There is an incredible smoothound fishery here. On the 13th July I got an Irish specimen smoothound a fraction under 9lbs, and on the 20th July added another of 10lbs 2ozs. That made seven specimens, but I was three short of my target and did not know where the next one would come from.

My next chance came off Courtmacsherry fishing with skipper Mark Gannon aboard the *Lady Louise*, on the 21st of July, 2014. I was doing a magazine feature, so didn't get much time to fish. Mark did suggest though, that this ground was good for big cuckoo wrasse. With this in mind, but mainly just to get a few species for the camera, I elected to fish a two-hook adjustable rig with the bottom hook positioned right by the lead weight to keep the bait bouncing on the rock as the boat drifted along. I caught pollack, small coalfish, a small ling, pout and poor cod, but was also picking up some cuckoo wrasse. I was fishing shoulder to shoulder with Mike Hennessy, and as I brought up a biggish cuckoo wrasse he said, "That's close to a specimen!" We weighed it at 1lb 3ozs, an ounce under specimen weight, so returned it. Only some 20 minutes later, I was tripping the baits over the rocky seabed feeling for snags and bites, when I got the typical triple rattle from a cuckoo wrasse. I struck the fish, and gently bought it up through the water column. As it came to the surface it looked huge and Mike said, "That's a specimen, for sure!" And it was, weighing 1lb 6ozs ashore a couple of hours later. It was a great way to start a week's trip.

Some of my specimen fish were inevitably lucky, but some I'd fished hard for using experience I gathered over the many years of fishing. Lady luck was about to smile on me in major way and give me a fish I never thought I'd even see, let alone catch.

After a couple of days mullet fishing, Mike Hennessy and I were booked aboard the *Loch an Lasc*, a 36-feet catamaran owned and skippered by Tom Collins based near Union Hall, West Cork. I was scheduled to fish for blue shark for a magazine feature along

2 Hook Adjustable Rig

"Neoprene Tubing will slide under pressure so the hook swivels can be repositioned higher or lower"

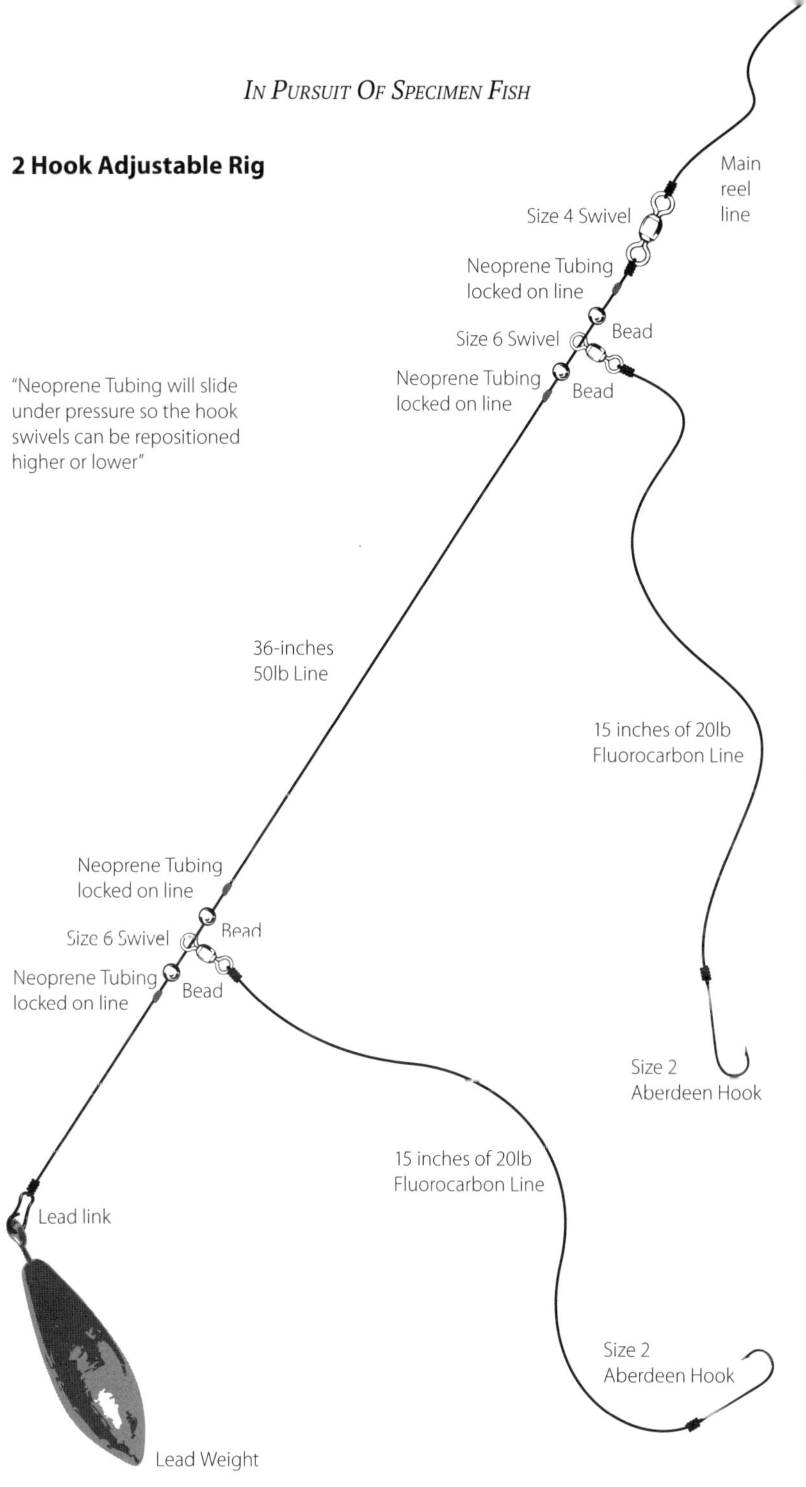

with two lads from Dublin. The day dawned sunny with a light southwest breeze, the sea flat calm. We headed out 16 miles in to 370-feet of water. The blues were on us straight away, and the lads I was fishing with both had virtually instant takes. I then got a blue about 90lbs, then dropped a shark that spat the bait. More sharks came to the other rods, then I hit a big fish that lengthen and girthed out at 120lbs.

I had been fishing fairly light tackle for the blue sharks, and was re-baiting with a small whole mackerel. I like to drop the bait over the side, let the bait fall in the water to extend the wire trace, then when all is sitting neat and tidy, let the balloon that suspends the bait in the water fall to the water and carry the bait away. As I did this with the new bait, I saw, in the speed of a lightening flash, a brown shape dart out from under the boat towards the bait, and turn straight back disappearing under the hull. I was speechless, my mind wondering if what I'd just seen was real. I already knew that stone basse, a fish found more in Mediterranean waters and on the very limit of their northern migration were caught in this quarter of Ireland, so identifying the fish was easy. The other guys were not aware of what had happened and I decided to keep quiet in case the fish had gone, never to be seen again.

It crossed my mind that the bait might be too big for it, also should I change to lighter tackle, but if I did this, the lapse in time might see the fish disappear. I put a mackerel fillet on to the hook, let the bait fall about five feet below the surface, then lifted the rod to make the bait lift a little. The brown shape reappeared, shot out from under the boat, grabbed the bait like it was its last meal, and bored back under the boat ripping line off the reel. The lads aboard looked round, and I said to Mike Hennessy, who is well aware of my quest for overall species, that I'd got a stone basse on and to get the net ready. This was a dogged fight, the fish reluctant to leave the the safety of the hull, me hanging over the gunnel with the rod near vertical, the tip deep under water trying to keep the line away from the hull to avoid abrasion, or it tangling with the propeller. In my head I knew this was probably the only time I'd ever hook a stone basse and was inwardly panicking in case I lost it. It took a few minutes to tire the fish, then it came out, wallowed on the surface, and was netted by Mike. What a tough, solid bodied, heavily scaled, almost prehistoric fish it looked. We weighed it aboard at over 9lbs, and it later weighed 9lbs exactly on accredited scales ashore later that evening. The qualifying Irish specimen weight was 8lbs, so lady luck, and that is exactly what that fish was, plain lucky, had given me a ninth specimen.

You learn in fishing that you go through periods when nothing goes right. Equally, at other times, you can't seem to put a foot wrong. When that occurs you have to push your luck as much as you can to see what happens. The week had already given me two specimens. Was there something more to come?

I needed a gilthead bream for my all time species count. I'd had a trip with Mike Hennessy and top species and specimen hunter Syd Kennedy on an estuary for gilthead back in 2010. We caught golden-grey mullet, then Syd and Mike both quickly got in to giltheads. It was non-stop action, and I was rushing round with the camera getting as many photos as possible for a feature I was compiling. By the time I'd got all the photos I needed, I grabbed a rod and put a bait in the water. The fish had already run through and the day was over. I'd missed my chance! I'd tried a few times elsewhere too, but it was always a case of "You should have been here yesterday", and the gilthead were just not playing ball with me.

It was Saturday 26th July. We had some work to do in the morning, but the afternoon was free, and it was my last day of what had been a great week. Mike said, What do you fancy doing for the last few hours?" I replied, "Gilthead!" We'd been based near Clonakilty for the week, and had tried for giltheads late one afternoon and one evening, but caught nothing and saw no sign of them. Other anglers fishing in the area were not catching either, and it seemed the gilthead were not there in any number and reluctant to show. For me, it was *deja vu*!

Working on the basis of 'if you don't try, you don't get', we elected to fish a small estuary in the area and Mike chose a pier that gave us casting access to the main channel. Low water came and went, Mike missed a small bite, but nothing was happening. We looked at each other and chose to move. Mike had a mark in mind, but when we got there, another angler was already wading in the water casting plugs for bass, so we needed another option.

I glanced to my left and way off in the distance noticed a small outcrop of rock that jutted out in to the main channel. "I fancy fishing there", I said to Mike, and he was quick to agree. By the time we walked to the outcrop, the tide was flooding quite quickly. The channel curved round the outcrop of rock, but 30 yards out there was a sandbank showing, and beyond that a shallow lagoon. Mike elected to cast in to the lagoon, but I fancied dropping a bait by the sandbank and letting the bait trot round with the tidal current.

I was concerned because the day was bright and sunny, and the water in the channel very clear and relatively shallow. I tackled up with a light mullet rod, a 4000-sized fixed spool reel loaded with 20lb braid, but added a short eight foot 20lb Fluorocarbon leader to the braid. I slid on a 1.5- ounce ball-weight, then a 5mm bead on to the Fluorocarbon, tied on a small swivel, then tied on 20 inches of 12b Fluorocarbon to the swivel, and added a size two Aberdeen hook to the end of the 12lb Fluorocarbon. The bait was a small fresh lugworm. I dropped the bait just in front of the sandbank, left the bait there for a few minutes, then decided to re-bait.

I was aiming to get the casts to drop on top of the sandbank, then draw in a little line to pull the weight and bait back to the incline of the bank, then let the tide push the bait down and round in to the deeper main channel. The tide was picking up and I felt the weight roll down the banks incline, sit for a few seconds, then occasionally roll along the bed of the channel a few inches. When it stopped I propped the rod in the rod rest and watched the rod tip. Suddenly the rod shivered and the tip pulled right over, the butt lifting off the ground. I grabbed the rod and struck, the whole rod buckling over, and whatever was on the other end took off dragging line of the screeching reel and forcing me to apply side pressure to try and turn the fish. Mike shouted, "It's your giltie, it's your giltie", and inwardly I cursed him as it just added more pressure to an already electric situation. The fish bored off right, then came back left, then went right again. I felt the line touch something, but pressure kept the fish moving. I was conscious of the light 12lb hook length, but needed to boss this fish as much as possible. The fish went right again, then doubled back, me reeling as fast as I could to maintain contact. The fish

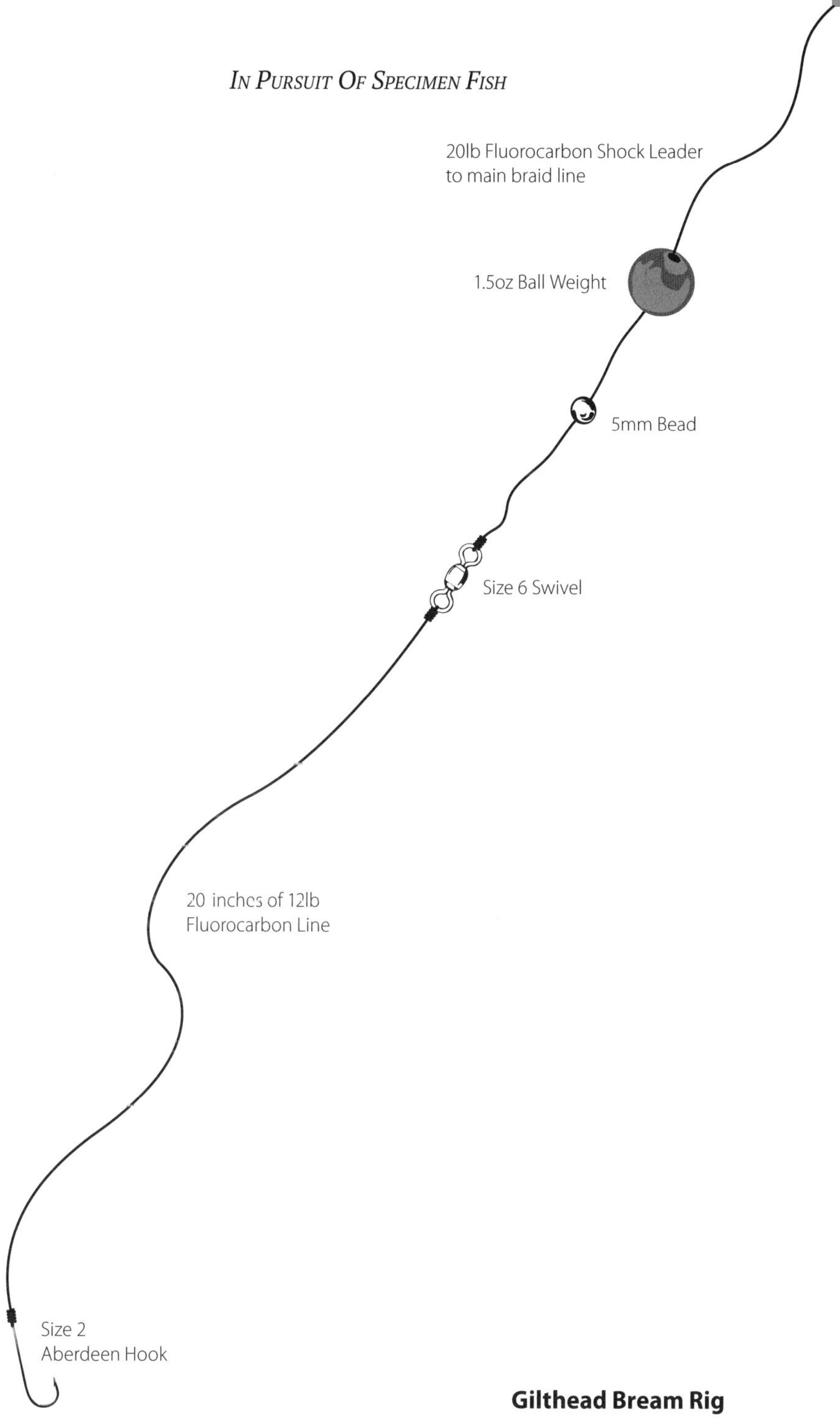

Gilthead Bream Rig

got a little slack and buried its head deep in to a weed covered rock ledge. I kept hard pressure on, the line literally singing, then the fish came out and bored off again. It was tiring now, but still very powerful. It went for the rock ledge again, but I managed to steer it away. I kept the pressure on then bullied the fish over the rock ledge and through the weed. It was in front of me now, and for the first time I saw that it was indeed a gilthead bream, and a big one. It dragged a few yards of line off to the left and right, then wallowed on the surface. This was my chance. I lifted the rod and watched the fish slide ashore, its spiked dorsal fin still defiant in defeat. What an amazing looking fish. Blue, green and silver scaled, with the tell-tale golden band above the eyes. I was shaking, flushed with adrenalin. It needed to weigh 3.08lbs to be a specimen. We weighed the fish at 4lb 3ozs. Not only had I added a new species, but got a hatrick of Irish specimen fish within the week. It was also my tenth official specimen, so I'd also achieved my long coveted 10 specimen badge.

The following day, heading back for the ferry, my mind wandered to all the years before when I first started to chase both species and specimen-sized fish. My instinct that I needed to maintain personal motivation and give myself these little targets had proved to be one of the main fishing driving forces. It had pushed me in to areas I would not otherwise have ventured. My choice was a personal path, and I'm glad I chose it to be so, for its given me experiences in angling I could not even have dreamed of when a small boy so long ago, eager to fish, but so often without the means or opportunity to actual go and wet a line.

Saltwater is in my veins, but occasionally I take a sip of freshwater to satisfy my will to fish, as we'll see in the next chapter.

Chapter 9
A Fresh Approach

I questioned myself about adding this chapter on freshwater fishing, and whether it was the right thing to do. The vast majority of my written work for magazines has been about saltwater fishing. Apart from my friends, few realise that my interest in fishing is all encompassing. My passion and addiction is angling, any angling, and I find it impossible to whittle out one discipline from another. I do not get to fish freshwater that much, but when I do I really enjoy it. Besides I wanted to add as many freshwater species to my all time species count as I could, but in doing that also found that learning new techniques for freshwater allowed me to rethink and better some of the methods I used in sea fishing. It is, therefore, exactly the right thing to do, for it is part of me, what I do, what I love, and what has helped to make me.

I caught my first trout in the small streams that flow off the rugged terrain of Cader Idris and the mountain lakes that adorn the base of her ice carved and then weather beaten face. A local man, a farm hand by trade, showed me how to fish the small streams, some so narrow you could literally stride across them in one single step. Surely there could not be fish in such small water? There were, and lots of them! He fished with a long length of bamboo with light monofilament line simply tied to one end with just a hook and a brandling worm dug from the chicken manure heap in the farm yard for bait. He would lift the cane, flick the worm forward, and let it trundle naturally with the current to seek out the hidden trout. He would pause, I would see the line tremble, then he would lift a lively wriggling trout from the water and drop it on the bank. He would take the trout for his breakfast, and why not. He showed me where the trout would lay. Look at the edge of the white water, where the current disappears under the banks, and where the water falls in to a pool. He was right, always! The trout were never more than eight to ten inches long, often smaller, but vivid with flanks of burnished gold, flashed with russet and crimson, and dotted with delicate spots. I never caught as many as he did, but I caught more than my share, because of what he showed me.

I ventured far in to the mountains to fish the high mountain lakes. They were hard waters to fish, troubled by bad weather, cold winds and short seasons. They were full of trout. Again mainly small, but sometimes a monster close to a pound would pull the float deep under, or grab a spinner as if it was its last meal, and in those waters there is minimal food, so little time for the trout to ponder the right and wrong of a bait, spinner or fly. I fished the River Treweryn near Bala and caught my first trout on the fly rod. An experience that left a feeling of awe inside me. But it was to end abruptly when the salt fully entered my veins, and my obsession with sea fishing ran away with me.

When we first came to Wales to live, there was a small river not far from Machynlleth I used to fish. It was similar to the small streams below Cader Idris in character, but in one part the river left a flat river bottom and entered a deep, narrow gorge. There was a sheep path along the gorge on the north side, overhung with trees and a steep 30 foot drop to the water. The river here was fast forcing itself through the gorge, but with several deep pools. Once, when walking the path, the bank suddenly gave way under my feet and I was left hanging by my arms from a tree root with thin air below and then the fast running water strewn with boulders. My rod was in the swirling pool below. I managed to get a leg over another root and inch my way to safety. I was not yet 16, and if my parents had known what had happened I fear they would never have let me near the river again. I never told them, but was far more careful on the path from there on in. Oh, and I got my rod back too, by hooking it with a cord and hook I fashioned out of fence wire.

Although the middle of the gorge was not accessible at all, the first two pools at the down river end of the gorge were, in low water conditions, just about navigable. The trout I usually caught from the river where smaller fish of just a few ounces, but good fun. I knew, if there were better fish available, that they would be in the deeper pools where nobody ever went. I bided my time until the river ran low, then made my way carefully up the north side of the gorge, inching along under the high bank and towering trees above, to the first pool. It was slippy underfoot and I went down several times, trying not to spook any fish, nor cast a forward shadow. I had a short eight feet fly rod and a centre-pin reel with 3lb line on. Baiting with a small lobworm I flicked the worm towards where the white water tumbled in to the pool forming a line of froth. There was a hint of darker, deeper water just off to the right and, after a few casts to the white water, I dropped the worm in to the deeper hole. I felt the trout pick up the worm and turn back for its lair. As the rod lifted the trout tore off, sulked in the deeper water, then turned and ran across the pool. For a second I thought it was gone, then felt the fish again as it headed flat out for the tail of the pool coming close to my feet. It turned again and headed back for the deep hole. I slowly kept the pressure on and guided the fish, tiring now, in to the centre of the pool and let it fight it out there. When spent, I led it ashore and threw myself on top of it. It was the biggest river trout I'd ever seen locally from the tiny brooks I fished. Weighed at home it went 1lb 1oz, had a small kype on the lower jaw, and the remains of a shrew in its stomach. A real cannibal that had ruled the pool for many summers.

During my time as a tackle consultant with Leeda Ltd in the mid and late 1990s, Nick Young, who was one of the brand product development team, offered to take me coarse fishing a few times. We were due to go on the River Wye, 22nd September, 1999, but constant rain prior to the trip got us wondering if fishing would even be possible. A quick phone call to Woody's Tackle Shop shop in Hereford suggested the river would be high, but still fishable, and "Yes, it was well worth a try." When we got there the river was high, in fact very high, and the colour of cocoa. Yet, as Woody had said, it was fishable, just about. We were targeting barbel and the knack was to cast across river, anchor a big feeder for as long as possible before weed and grass collected on the line and swept the feeder, and bait, away. As I sat there, I watched tree trunks, branches, then a dead cow float past. Could you really catch fish in this? While observing I noticed a bulge in the surface water upstream of me near the far bank. This was obviously a submerged rock lying up above the bulge and I figured that maybe a barbel or two might be using this to break the fast flowing current. This was my kind of technique, pretty much the same as uptide casting off the boat. I loaded the feeder and hammered the cast up river of the surface showing bulge. As soon as the feeder settled, I released line to form a bow and pull the feeder back in a direct line, much like an anchor rope. It settled and held, fixed in position by the direct pull of the line downstream of it. This increased my fishing time by a good couple of minutes. I started to catch chub, dace, then a couple of small barbel, my very first ever in fact. I kept picking up the odd barbel, but then I saw the rod tip pull straight and the line start falling back. I struck expecting it to be just weed on the line, but felt an almighty kick on the rod tip and a decent fish bore for the riverbed. This fought head down, lunging, but did not run, until I got it near my own bank. Now it took off down river, trying to get to some tree roots. It turned and came back upriver. It was soon tired though, and I netted a barbel that proved to weigh 9lbs 2ozs. Not a huge fish, but back then it was a nice way to start barbel fishing. I fished a few other venues catching bream, crucian carp, common carp, perch and tench during the occasional trips over the next few years.

I came back in to freshwater fishing more regularly by chance. Isn't a life change so often by chance? I'd worked as a contributor on the radio programme *Dirty Tackle* presented by Nick Fisher and produced by Helen Stiles during the 90's. When *Dirty Tackle* came to end, Helen was keen to format a new angling programme. The pitch to the BBC was successful and *Fish On Five* airing on BBC Radio 5 Live was commissioned. It would be presented by Nick Hancock, a well-known comedian and TV presenter, but would feature three anglers who would accompany Nick on his adventures. For coarse fishing it was Andy Little, a long time angling journalist and tackle consultant, also Jon Beer, again an angling journalist and expert fly fisherman who would cover game fishing. I was to do all things saltwater, but the show would see us all mix in together and swap disciplines.

The show proved very popular, even with its 6am time slot on a Saturday morning. We, as a collective, had many adventures together and I caught my best pike, a near 20lber on a lure at Hampton Court on the Thames, also fly caught pike while recording the show. We also went to the Sway fishery in Hampshire targeting big roach, and with some great coaching from Andy, I caught several 2lb-plus roach including a 2lb 6oz fish, a fish of a lifetime that will be hard to ever beat. While fishing a lake in Surrey, with Nick, Andy and Helen at one end, and me on the other end of the lake, I noticed to my left a patch of lily pads. I could see occasionally that the pads were moving as fish underneath disturbed them. I crawled round on my hands and knees, careful not to disturb them. Hiding behind a small bush, I put a piece of bread on the hook, dipped it in the water to add a little weight, and dropped the crust underhand in to a small clear patch between the lily pads. Five minutes later a huge mouth appeared under the crust, sucked it in, and all hell broke loose, the fish charging off, then doubling back in to the pads. It fought it out in amongst weeds, but became stuck with the line inbetween the stalks of the lily's. Andy was with me like a shot, and it was a case of taking the valuables out of your pockets and going in after the fish, wet trousers and all, in up to the waist. We got it loose and after a few minutes fight we netted a cracking-looking 22lb mirror carp. One of the most memorable carp I've had in the UK. I also went to fish a lake in France for carp and added fish of 24lbs 13ozs, 32lbs 2ozs and 36lbs 2ozs to my list. Again by carp standards nowadays, nothing amazingly big, but these fish, to me, were something special at the time and taught me a lot. I've also fished the River Ebro in Spain for the catfish, and caught, but not the 100lb fish I would have liked.

I went back to fly fishing around 2002. I'd missed it. There are times when the spring and summer sea fishing is hard, and sometimes I need a change to recharge my batteries. The fly rod is a good healer. I rarely target the big pellet fed trout, though that can be fun occasionally. I prefer to fish the wild mountains lakes for their peace, quiet and beauty. It is my thinking time, my time out from an often too-fast working life, when I ponder where things are, where I stand, how I should react to situations, and think through possible solutions.

I like the fly. It is thinking fishing. I rarely if ever pull lures. I fish trying to represent the insects on the water. It is finding the solution to a fishing problem that I like the best, and on my mountain waters the fishing is never easy and problems common place. I don't fish to catch fish, as such. I truly don't! A catch is a bonus. It is the take of the trout to the fly that I fish for. The rod, inanimate in your hand one second, and a nanosecond later it's hit by a train dragging the rod tip over and forcing you to give line through the fingers. I often just stand and observe. I'm looking for trout feeding, not just rising, but bulging the surface water as they take emergers just under the surface. If I see a fish feeding, I cast to it. To predict where a moving fish will head, present the fly to it, see the water bulge, then feel the rod tip drag over is an incredible feeling that once experienced makes you want it more and more. Native browns are good on the dry fly in summer, but I also like an overwintered rainbow that will leap clear of the water several times and tail dance in mid air when feeling the hook. I do not discriminate. Why should you? Both are fun, different, but equal as an adversary.

Sea trout and salmon I want to fish for more. I've caught both and its awakened a hunger to repeat the experience. The take of a seatrout on the fly on a moonless night is special. My salmon have only been small grilse so far, but I've listened to anglers who have hooked and landed double figure and bigger salmon on the fly, and its a life event I need to live. As an angler, how could you leave a fish of such magic distinction vacant on your all time list!

Its now time to look further afield to waters bathed by a warm sun and filled full of dreamtime fish.

Chapter 10
The Florida Keys

All anglers have dreams. In the beginning it's just to catch fish, then a big fish, and in all probability to then catch lots of big fish. The ultimate dream though, for most, is to fish for exotic fish in warm waters far far away. I'd long read of the Florida Keys, its waters holding a plethora of big, hard-fighting species. Its fishing hub was Islamorada, often quoted as the 'Sports Fishing Capital Of The World'. As early as the 1990s I'd set my heart on fishing there someday.

It was April of 1999. My friend and often work colleague, Rob Wyatt, and I were having a beer one night when the topic of far off places, and species such as sailfish, bonefish, bull sharks and giant stingray came in to the conversation. The words flowed easily, as did the beer, and by the time the evening drew to a close, we were planning a trip to the mecca of sport fishing, Islamorada. We chose November, as we wanted to try and catch a sailfish each, and this is the start of the sailfish season, but also factored in were the big bull sharks, bonefish, and just about anything else we could target. Our plan was to hire an offshore game fishing boat for two days, along with a flats boat for two days, to sample both offshore and inshore fishing. The rest of the time would be spent fishing the shore, wherever possible, for whatever came along.

Never was a trip so meticulously planned. Well, some of it. Whenever we could get together we discussed at length the right rods, reels and terminal tackle to take. I made up traces, packed, unpacked and repacked gear so many times I lost count, this to get the luggage weight within the airline restriction. Reels were stripped and rebuilt, rods triple checked for any signs of wear, and suitable clothes were bought. The motel accommodation was booked online. It looked good, and was right alongside a waterway, and that meant we could fish almost straight out of the motel room door. Inevitably, like kids, we were ready to go weeks before our departure date...time passing oh so very slowly. Eventually, I was in the car, heading to Rob's, then on to Heathrow for the flight out to Miami.

Arriving in Miami, we had no problems picking up the hire car. All, so far, had gone to plan. We left Miami and headed down the Turnpike towards The Keys, counting the mile-marker posts, bursting with anticipation. Life though can reign you in all to easily. We arrived at the motel. At reception was a scruffy looking lady and a rather plump man sat in a torn t-shirt. He looked like he hadn't washed for a month. I sensed we may have made a mistake straight away. We got the key and went to the apartment. It was not what we expected, nor was it as it appeared in the online advertisement. It was dirty, smelt of damp, and the bathroom was filthy. Now I'm not posh in any shape or form, and will happily live the rough life as and when needed, but I have to be clean...and this was not clean at all. Rob looked a bit shocked when I flatly refused to stay there. He felt much the same though, it was just that he knew me well and I'm usually the last to complain. We made the decision to go back to reception, explain it was not what we expected, which we did, and surprisingly they were suspiciously understanding and accepted our decision without question. It was now 8.30 in the evening and we had no where to stay, a hire car full of luggage and tackle. We were also hungry and very tired.

We were both aware of the Cheeka Lodge. A hotel renowned for its popularity with anglers including the likes of former US President George Bush Snr, scores of hollywood stars, race drivers and numerous other celebrities too numerous to mention. It was though, for us at the time a bit pricey and we'd decided on the motel as the cheapest option allowing us to get more fishing in. We discussed our now dire situation. I suggested that we investigate the Cheeka Lodge, and if affordable book in for just for one night, reassess our situation, then take it from there. We pulled in to the Cheeka Lodge car park, and I walked towards the main lobby entrance. The Concierge spoke a greeting and we engaged in conversation. I told him we did not have a booking, but wondered if there were vacancies, and as I did this, also dropped a $10 note in to his hand. It was one of the best $10 I've ever spent. He could not do more for us. He whispered something to the lady at reception, and it turned out that they would do a deal for three nights that was very affordable, but then we would have to leave as there was a major NASCAR event in the area and the hotel was then fully booked. Three nights sorted. The following day we booked in to a motel, after wisely viewing the rooms, for the remainder of our trip and all was well. Well sort of! Rob had borrowed a rather expensive, state-of-the-art fly rod, and while taking the rod out of the bag and checking things over, managed to insert the top of the tip section in to the ceiling fan....which promptly chopped it off. I didn't get involved in that one. It was Rob's problem to sort!

Our first boat trip, on the 8th November, was with a famous captain and angler, Skip Nielsen, working out of Bud 'n Mary's marina in Islamorada. It was a very windy day with the sea rough. Skip initially thought we were 'tourist' anglers and was doubtful of going out incase we were not up to the job. We explained we were desperate to fish and had come a long way. He asked where we were from, and when I said, "the UK", he asked if I ever fished the North Sea. I said I did, and often, and he replied, "Hell, come on, we'll go!". Such is the reputation of the angry North Sea, it was our saviour on the day. We went out to the famous mark known as 'The Humps' off Islamorada and caught yellowtail, cero mackerel, kingfish and yellowjack. We also fished whole small fish dropped deep down on to the rough ground and took nassau grouper to over 20lbs. We both had hard-fighting amberjack to 40lbs too, these turning back hard for the seabed several times during the fight. We had another day booked with Skip and this would be for sailfish.

The next day the weather was worse, but we were due to go out with Drew Moret working from the marina at nearby Lorelei. Again Drew was worried about us, and the weather, but we explained, as before, we were true anglers and ultra-keen to fish. It was a hard day. I had a black tip shark on a plug, and we both took barracuda, grunts, mangrove snapper, and other smaller species, but the flats were milked up and just not fishing well. In two days we would be out with Drew again and we asked about the possibility of targeting sharks. Now the flats captains, at the time, were not too keen on going for the sharks, but our persuasive conversation saw him agree to trying for the sharks, if the weather had settled down enough. He suggested, that with us being out with Skip Nielsen the next day, that we ask Skip to target barracuda for the last hour and bring a couple of these with us for bait with strict instructions to keep them cool over night. We finished the day fishing off the pier at the Cheeka Lodge catching numerous grunts, small barracuda, and snappers, while eating fried chicken and drinking chilled white wine.

The next day saw an improvement in the weather, with a light breeze and settling sea. We headed out with sailfish in mind. Our crewman, Ben, showed us how to mount the small pilchards on the small 2/0 sized hooks, then these were then flicked out freeline about 30 to 40 yards. One rod had the line placed in the outrigger clip, leaving you free to watch and wait in hopeful anticipation. Another was dropped in to a rod holder on the gunnel with the line held in a makeshift clip and the fixed spool reel in free spool.

I was stood on the port side looking aft when the outrigger next to me 'thwanged' as the line clip gave to the increased line tension. A sailfish had taken the pilchard and was heading off for deeper water. I struck exactly as indicated to...the fish was there momentarily, but then was gone. The hook came back bare. Rob then missed a bite, but then hooked and caught a sailfish about 20lbs. It was one of the most beautiful fish we'd ever seen. We were both elated, but were keen to get the fish back and watched it slip away with just a couple of tail swipes.

Rob almost immediately caught another sailfish about 35lbs, then I missed another pull, again resulting in an empty hook. What was happening was that the sailfish took the pilchard, felt the hook, leapt free from the water shaking their heads, and twice I'd seen the hook fly out of their mouth as they were airborne. It suggested I was not giving the fish long enough to eat the bait before striking.

The next take I was ready for. I was literally watching the pilchard, which I could occasionally see flash in the water. I suddenly became aware of what looked like moving brown seaweed behind the pilchard. The dull seaweed suddenly lit up in blues, silvers and green, a long bill poked free from the water thrashing side to side, and I literally watched in awe as a mouth appeared behind the pilchard and it was sucked straight in. On this rod, instead of the line held in the outrigger clip, the line was held under tension clipped inside a short, soft length of copper wire attached to the rod, which as the fish took the pilchard, the line would pull free from the wire, leaving line free to spill from the open spool of the fixed spool reel. Even so there was no mistaking the *ping* as the line came free from the wire, and the *swish* as line left the spool. I grabbed the rod and initially let line spill off the reel spool. I counted to five, flipped the bale-arm over, then struck. I felt weight, and this time the fish was on. It went straight off across the surface behind the boat, fin initially erect, then flat. Its head went down and ripped line off the reel. It twisted and turned, then came straight up vertically clearing the water with its tail and head thrashing side to side. It was like slow motion, I can remember seeing water streaming off its sides as it was clear of the surface and fully airborne. The sailfish leapt three more times, then went deep. It circled for a couple of minutes, then tired. Easing it closer to us, Ben grabbed first the leader, then the fish at the side of the boat and gently lifted her aboard. It was estimated to weight about 30lbs and was released after a photo. I caught another fish straight after that weighed about 20lbs, but missed at least six or seven other takes on the day. It mattered not. We both had our sailfish. It was my first ever billfish, and something, as a child, I never thought I'd ever get the chance to fish for. The last hour we caught two barracuda about 8lbs each, which we took back in a cool box ready for the shark trip the next day.

Again the weather had improved, the flats water being less milky, and the breeze just a light one from the south. It was hot and we piled on the sun cream to avoid burning. Our flats captain,

Drew, suggested that he would take us out to a sand flat, then anchor up putting us within casting range of a deeper channel. The sharks were in the channel. Drew cut the fillets off the barracuda and hung the body in the water off the stern of the boat to attract the sharks. However he added that, "Usually the sharks are always there, the body of the barracuda is just back up. Cast out and expect a take straight away". Shark fishing in the UK is a waiting game, and being naive at the time, Rob and I were both sceptical of this sweeping statement and exchanged doubting glances.

We were using light spinning tackle with just 15lb mono line. The leader was piano wire, and the hook a small size 4/0. You cut a four-inch by four-inch square of thick flesh and skin from the fillet of the barracuda, passed the hook once through one corner, then simply cast this in to the channel a few yards away to fish free-line. Rob and I were side by side and cast simultaneously. I watched my bait splash down on the surface noisily. You hold the rod to feel for bites, but leave the reel with the bale-arm open so that when shark takes, it can run freely as it carries the bait off.

I turned to Rob to say something, and as I did so, felt line start to trickle off the spool. I watched as the speed of the line leaving the spool increased. I let the fish run about 20 yards, then flipped the bale-arm over, lifted the rod and waited for the increasing pressure to pull the hook home. The fish felt the hook, turned for the deeper channel water, and immediately took a lot of line from me. It swung around, swam up and down the channel a few times, then went on a very long run dragging maybe 50 yards or more of line off the reel. It was a hard-fought battle, the shark was a stubborn, methodical fighter. It came towards the boat four or five times, but each time, seen just as a brown blur, it turned and headed away. It took 45 minutes to get it to us. It was a bull shark about 100lbs in weight. They leave the fish in the water and just cut the trace to release the shark as there is no way you can really bring a fish of this size and power in to what is a relatively small boat, and I watched it melt away to nothing.

Immediately we both re-baited and cast again. I watched the slab of barracuda fly out and splash on the surface. I let line feed off the spool allowing the bait to sink. I was just wondering how deep the channel was when I realised that something had taken the bait on the drop and was starting to run off with it. I let it run, run a little more, then flipped the bale-arm over and waited for that satisfying tension a rod takes on as it bends in to a good fish. The rod kept bending, and bending, then line poured off the reel, the reel fizzing as it did so. I was instantly aware this was a much bigger fish. It was in the channel and heading south fast. It took maybe 100 yards of line, then pressure turned it briefly, but it turned back and went for the south again, and faster. I was concerned I would run out of line, but Drew was thinking the same and pulled free the push-pole that was holding us in place.

The shark kept going, the boat was being dragged in to the main channel, and the fish just would not stop. I remember glancing at the reel and seeing no more than 30 yards of line left on the spool. I piled as much pressure as the 15lb line would allow, and gradually the fish slowed and sulked in the channel. I gained line, the shark would take it back. I'd gain line, the shark would take it back. This is how it was for over an hour. Neither of us would give anything easily. I felt the shark slow and go deep to the bottom of the channel. I kept the pressure on and was able to gain quite a bit of line by lifting the rod to pull the fish towards me, then dropping the rod and retrieving a few inches of line at a time. The shark was now maybe 75 yards away, but it found a second wind and swam fast and consistently away from me taking another 75 yards of line with it. I got that back in the next five minutes, then it went again. After about one hour and 45 minutes, the shark was some 50 yards off the stern. I really had to pile the pressure on now and after another five minutes got the fish nearly to the boat. It was a big bull shark, much, much bigger than the last, round bellied and heavy behind the head. They are not called bulls for nothing. They are stubborn, powerful and will not be easily lead. It came to the boat a half dozen times, stayed deep, and would just turn and swim away again.

With over two hours now gone it was time for one last effort. Using all the rod and line power I had I forced the shark up and towards me, foot by foot. A brown blur looked up from the coloured water. First its brutish head, then its fin and tail broke surface. I manoeuvred it to the side of the boat, Drew reached out, grabbed the wire leader and held the shark at the side of the boat. Rob tried to get a photo, but as Drew held it and I put my hand on the dorsal fin, the fish thrashed its head, the hook straightened and the fish, free at last, turned for the channel and was gone. I asked Drew what he thought it weighed. It was comfortably 200lbs and could, given the size of its belly girth, have been closer to 250lbs. Even at 200lbs it was my very first 10 to 1 fish, a caught fish ten times heavier than the line breaking strain used. Our week away ended with Rob catching bonefish to 9lbs and an incredible permit that bounced 35lb scales down to the limit, with me getting bonnethead sharks, jack crevalle and a host of other new species.

LET'S TALK TARPON

Another fish I read avidly about as a boy were tarpon. Tales told of giant fish and long fights were enough to fire and hold an interest that would stay with me for over three decades. Rob was of the same persuasion and we organised another trip to The Keys in 2004 to try and achieve our tarpon dream.

It was May, and what should have been great weather and peak tarpon time was anything but. The weather was unseasonably cold, with strong and persistent east winds and cooler than normal sea temperatures. The reports immediately prior to our trip where not good with barely any tarpon taken and no real sign of things improving. We went out with the intention of trying for tarpon anyway, but would also fish sharks, stingrays, and for whatever else we could target. We would be fishing with a dry humoured, joke-cracking New Yorker, Izzy Donatelli. He was a great captain with immense experience, but you never knew whether he was being serious or not, which kept you on your toes. He ran two boats out from Robbie's Marina in Islamorada. We also took more care and booked a better motel with sea front access for fishing from at night off the shore.

When we arrived, we went straight to Robbie's Marina. Here you can feed resident tarpon by hand right underneath the boat pontoons, but even here the numbers of tarpon were not as high as normal. Our captain, Izzy, said it was going to be hard, but we would try our best. There had only been one tarpon from the area the previous week. We fished the first day, the 13th of May, looking for tarpon and seeing nothing. We caught a few sharks, mainly nurse shark, but also a couple of decent lemon sharks around 100lbs. Izzy suggested that the second day, instead of fishing through the day, he thought we would stand a much better chance fishing in the dark over low water and the early flood tide. He knew where he wanted to fish as well, a mark not far from the Indian Key channel, and towards the island.

The night of the 14th it was so cold I wore a t-shirt, sweat shirt, in addition to a thick fleece coat. With hindsight jeans would have been better than the shorts I was wearing. The Keys were proving to be much colder than normal! We motored out as the last light was fading and were anchored up as dusk fully fell. Izzy suggested we should float fish small swimming crab at a depth of about six feet. The hook is positioned in the corner edge of the crabs shell with the point prominent so that the hook has the maximum chance to get a good hold.

It was eerie sitting out on the flats at night. The lights of the towns twinkling like little stars down the coast, a pale moon doing its best to smile through a thin cloud base, and the unnerving splash of small fish skittering on the surface periodically. We could not see the floats. The tactic was to trickle the float away from the boat about 50 yards using the tide to sit the baits over a slightly deeper channel that Izzy expected the tarpon to swim through. The reels were set on a very light drag, just enough to allow the tarpon to take the crab and run without feeling undue line or rod pressure.

Occasionally we heard, out in the distance, a noise that sounded like *cloop*. Izzy said it was tarpon taking in air. I was sat there, concentrating. I was not prepared for what happened next. I was holding the rod across my body pointing towards the back of the boat. Sometimes I could just feel the pull of the float on the line as the tidal current and swell made the float bob. The take, when it came, I can best describe as savage. The reel was silent, then a nanosecond later it was giving out a high pitch scream, screaming so loud it hurt. It was like taking a F1 V8 750hp engine from tick-over to 18,000 revs in a split-second. I lifted the rod, put my finger on the spool to add a little more drag, and set the hook. The fish was a long way away already and hammered the rod right over. It went to the right, then doubled back left. I could see nothing but felt the line lifting in the water and said to Rob, "Its going to jump!" Somewhere out in the near inky blackness, we heard a huge splash. My tarpon, for a couple of seconds, was partially or wholly airborne. Now it ran fast, doubled back and went to my right, pulled stoically against the rod then bored off to the left. I was inching line back on the reel a little bit at a time, but then losing it again.

The cold night air now seemed somewhat warmer and sweat was trickling down my temples. I felt the fish lift in the water and maybe 40 to 50 yards behind the boat we saw white water as it broached. I could feel the fish tiring now, but it was still powerful and would make short runs often doubling back on itself. I eased the drag off slightly, just in case the fish turned and ran under pressure when getting close to the boat. We saw another surge of white water, now just 25 yards away. The fish then went deep and was maybe 10 to 15 feet below the boat. I worked the fish hard using the 20lb line to its maximum effect. Slowly, just ever so slowly, the fish was coming up. Suddenly it showed on the surface, rolled and stayed on its side. It was beaten. Izzy grabbed the leader and held it at the side of the boat. It was my choice to release the fish as fast as possible. Rob tried to get me a photo, but while we looked at the fish I did ease out a single scale as a memento. I'm glad I did as the photo unfortunately did not come out in the dark. I felt the flank of the fish, then as Izzy held the head and I held the body, we turned the fish away from the boat, held her there, and after a few seconds she voluntarily swam slowly from our grasp. Izzy said the fish was around 120lbs in weight. It was a big fish and heavy behind the head as all big fish are. An hour later, after we both missed bites, Rob got a tarpon about the same size. We both had our dream fish, and against all the odds we were later told, for those were the only confirmed tarpon that week within that area. We spent the rest of the trip catching lemon sharks to 110lbs, nurse sharks to 130lbs, stingray to 100lbs, but losing much bigger ones, and a host of other species. We saw no more tarpon!

This segment on tarpon proves the point how important a good captain or skipper is to the success of the angler. It's all too easy to forget that both parties need each other. It was Izzy's knowledge of the area and where he thought the tarpon would be that proved vitally important on the night. It was our job to not let him down and fight and play the fish correctly and to the best of our ability to ensure a successful capture. If you find a good skipper, look after him. Do your best to nurture a good working relationship, and it will pay you back ten fold!

My next adventure was to a place I never thought I'd go, and when asked, knew little about: The Gambia!

Chapter 11 Gambia

I was working on a magazine feature at my desk one day in August, 2000. The phone rang. It was Richard Sheard of *World Sport Fishing*. He asked if I'd be interested in a trip to The Gambia to do some magazine features. I was also working for *Fish On 5* on BBC Radio 5 Live at the time, so I would also be recording segments for the show while in The Gambia. Rob Wyatt would come over with me to handle sound issues and get some extra photography for me.

We were due to travel out on the 30th September. The first few days to be a mix of small boat and beach fishing, then we would motor east up the Gambia River to McCarthy Island, somewhere where little if any rod and line fishing had ever been done, then drive back to the coast and fish from small boats for a couple of days to get a full feel for the place, and to gauge the overall fishing potential.

We were staying at a place called African Village. The beach in front of the hotel, and nearby Leybato beach, proved to be good for shore fishing at night producing fish called sunpat, best described as a heavily built bream like fish, also tundara rays, and thick-lipped grouper. In daylight I caught guitarfish to just under 20lbs, catfish, and more grouper. We also fished from small 16-foot boats some two to three miles offshore. On one trip we drift fished from sand on to a rocky edge and I added a 17lb cassava to my species count, which was building quickly. In the mangroves, fishing in just a few feet of water, I caught small snapper-like fish, also frog fish and multi coloured banded eels.

The preliminaries out of the way, we loaded up two Land Rovers, and headed up the south side of the Gambia River. This was, as I remember, a near 300-mile one-way trip. It was good to see Gambia from the road, or what passed as a road in some places, and it gave me an insight in to this diverse country. While travelling I noticed that the only livestock were goats. I saw no cows, neither going there, nor heading back. We pulled in to a small village where we were due to eat. The menu, written in broken English on a ragged piece of paper said, quite simply, beef stew. There was no other option. The stew was served with a rice-based dish called benachin, sometimes referred to as jollof rice. It is mixed with tomatoes, tomato paste, onions, salt, ginger, cumin, peppers and other ingredients. These combine to turn it a light orange colour. It is delicious and was just that served alongside the 'beef' stew. I was sat opposite one of our group when he casually said, "It's pretty good, this beef!" I replied back, very matter of fact, that I'd seen no cows on the journey, only goats. He paused just prior to putting the next forkful in his mouth, then turned white as he realised the consequences of what I'd just said, and put the fork back down. I pointed out that goat is a staple part of the diet in many parts of the world, and also mentioned that for the next four days, if he didn't eat goat, he was likely to go very hungry. This seemed to do the trick and by the second day he was getting stuck in as good as anyone.

Apart from a Land Rover breaking down a couple of times, which turned out to be first an electrical, then a fuel problem, the journey was fairly straightforward. We were literally staying in traditional African huts. The huts took two people, you slept on bunks, but there was a basic shower. It was set amongst a semi jungle setting with the river just 50 yards or so away. At night you fell asleep to the sounds of the Gambian scrub wild life all around you.

The majority of the group were scheduled to fish on a traditional pirougue, a narrow-hulled boat with a sun screen. There wasn't room for all of us, so with me having my own boat back in the UK, it was decided that Rob and I would take out a 10-foot dingy and fish from this. At this point, its worth mentioning that the width of the Gambia River locally was quite wide, some few hundred yards in places...oh, and there were crocodiles too! Though, as it turned out, this wasn't the only danger.

The first day we went looking for tigerfish. A small one was caught, but little else. On the way back from the tigerfish mark, I saw something ahead that looked like a large rock. It was difficult for me to see over the bow of the little boat, which was sitting a little high in the water. Rob said to steer right and it would be okay. As I lifted off the thwart (seat) at the stern of the boat to get a better look, the 'rock' launched itself out of the water like a missile and started swimming fast for shore. It was a hippo, a beast not to be messed with and responsible for many a missing tourist. It caused an alarming wave pattern that I had to throttle forward through, but luckily we made it. It was a close shave, and not the last as it turned out.

The river water temperature was very hot and the fishing seemed subdued, but we caught many different kinds of catfish including an electric catfish that can shock you with a charge of electricity if touched, and elephant fish that have a strange trunk shaped mouth. There are huge catfish in this river too, not dissimilar to vundu, and I hooked and lost a very large fish when fishing a small fish bait that hugged the bottom, but after a minute or so managed to break my line on a rock. There are many other species too, including fish we saw in saltwater back on the coast that seem to have adapted to the up river environment, such as captain fish and joto.

In the mornings, a couple of us would go down to a small wooden jetty where we would catch small characyns, little silver fish not dissimilar to thin shaped roach, for bait. The first morning, at the back of the jetty I noticed the head of a fish sticking out from a hole in the river bank. I could not see what it was, nor could I see how big it was. I tried to catch it, and though it showed some slight interest in the offered baits, it would not leave its lair. That following night the fish was still there, so then, and each following morning and evening, I dropped bits of bread down the edge of the jetty near its hole to gradually lure it out. It was reluctant, but now and then would partially come out to take some bread. I deliberately left the fish alone until the very last morning.

I was keen to catch this fish as it was totally different to everything else we had seen. I set up a small spinning rod with light 10lb mono, and simply added a size eight hook to the end of the line. I baited with bread, just a small chunk of white flake about the size of a small coin. This I dipped in the water, well away from the fish's hole, just to add a little weight to get it to drop down in the water in front of the fish. I knew exactly where the fish and its hole was, so crawled on my belly across the decking until the length of the rod would reach the water and positioned the bread in front of the fish. I gently lowered the bread in to the water, let it sink about 18 inches, then watched the line for a bite. Nothing happened for about a minute or so, then I saw the line shudder. I thought it might be one of the little characyns, but then the line darted back towards the fish's bank side hole and I struck.

It was a tug of war, the fish trying to get its body back in to the hole, and me trying to keep it out of there. I succeeded and the fish changed tactics by charging under the decking of the jetty trying to get round one of the supports. It then moved out in to deeper, more open water, before charging for the jetty again. The fish did not feel overly big, but it was fighting like a demon. It went deep, then bored right under the jetty again. I played it out and suddenly it just gave up and rolled on the surface. I lifted it in and was unsure exactly what it was. I thought it might be a tilapia as I knew these had been farmed in the region for food from the 1970s, and wondered if this might be an escapee. Richard also thought it was a tilapia. On arrival home, after the trip, it did indeed prove to be a tilapia and was an unusual and unexpected catch. Incidentally, the fish was returned alive to the water.

The characyns I'd been catching for bait were very slimy, leaving this slime all over your hands when handled. I'd got in to the habit, after catching a few, that I'd lay on my stomach at the end of the jetty, reach down with my arms, and wash my hands free of the slime. I was doing this on the very last morning when one of the local guides who had been helping us, ran on to the jetty behind me and started slapping his hands together, violently shaking his head, and indicating I should not wash my hands in the water. It turned out that the Gambia River is home to a sub species of the Nile crocodile, and a rather large specimen had been living under the jetty for quite some time. I marked that down as another lucky escape.

On the journey back, we dropped in to a jungle camp to eat. One of the guides suggested I should try the bush pig, as it was outstanding. Never one to shy away from trying new food, I did indeed order the bush pig. It was one of the best meals I've ever had. A slightly sweet roast pork that literally melted in the mouth. It was at this same camp they had captive crocodiles in a pool. A cat, trying to be clever, walked along the edge of the pool at what it thought was a safe distance. A clever croc, idling his time away in the cool water, suddenly launched itself out of the pool at incredible speed and grabbed the cat between its jaws. Such was the power of those jaws I doubt the cat felt a thing, but my mind turned back to the jetty, me washing my hands, and the nervous local. Also on the walls of the room we ate in was the saw shaped bill from a sawfish. The bill was at least seven to eight feet in length. I asked about the capture of this fish and it was caught in the river not far from the camp and was said to exceed 20 feet in length.

Arriving back at African Village, my last two days were to be spent on the small boats fishing for what the Gambians call captain fish. I'd done a little research on these prior to leaving the UK and recognised them straight away. They are basically the same fish as the Australian thread-fin salmon. They usually go between 30cm and 50cm in length and can weigh up to about 30lbs, though much bigger fish have been caught in Australia. The captain fish, at least the biggest ones are, are generally found around the sandbanks where the Gambia River enters the sea.

It was hot and very humid as we set out from Denton Bridge across the banks to reach the edge of the main channel. We anchored the boat and put small whole fish baits, called yahboys, downtide of the boat. The flow of the river had a major influence here, and I found, by reducing the amount of lead weight I used, that I could trot the bait down the channel until it came up against the rising incline of a shallow sandbank and would stay there. It wasn't long before I got a bite and struck in to a powerful fish that turned and ran with current, then hung very deep as I played it back to the boat. This was a captain fish about 20lbs.

The mouth on a captain fish is quite large, so I selected a bigger bait this time and trotted this well back of the boat. I was actually in the middle of doing a radio recording when I saw the rod tip shudder and start to pull round. I struck the fish and it instantly felt much heavier. It not only ran with the current, but went around a sandbank that was showing on the surface as rough water. It hung there keeping its head down and taking short bursts of line off the reel. All I could do was keep pressure on. The fish went left and I could do little about it bar for applying side pressure by dropping the rod to the right. Surprisingly the fish turned and swept past the shallow bank in to deeper and safer water. The fish would not tire and made numerous short runs, but I was slowly working it ever closer to the boat. The water under the boat was about 20 feet deep, and the fish just hung there using its weight to hug the bottom. I kept pressure on the fish and it slowly came up and turned over on its side just rear of the boat. The guide grabbed the fish and hauled it aboard. We weighed the fish at just over 40lbs. A big captain fish! I caught another about an hour later that judged against the 40lber was in excess of 35lbs. I followed that up with snapper over 20lbs and another big cassava the next day to end a quite remarkable trip.

I greatly enjoyed Gambia! They say Africa, as a continent and its spirit, gets under your skin. I would have to agree with that. Its laid-back lifestyle, friendly people, colourful dress, and bustling markets, and its fishing, made a serious impression on me. Like everywhere, since then I'm sure it has changed, but at the time of my visit it was a jewel, and a trip I will never forget.

It's time to head west again now, to the desert scenery of the Baja Peninsula in Mexico for some of the best fishing I've ever experienced.

Chapter 12
Mexico

Still flushed with the success of our Florida trip back in 1999, Rob Wyatt and I had been thinking of organising another trip to somewhere warm. I guess it was inevitable, but we both wanted to catch a marlin. Our problem was money, more the lack of it. We didn't have the resources to just book a venue noted for 1000lb marlin. Our intention was just to catch a marlin, any marlin, and this would be dictated by the overall cost of the trip. Much research was done between us, identifying then eliminating venues on a basis of cost and consistency of catches. Finally one destination stood out as being affordable giving us several days offshore, but also where the catches of marlin proved very consistent, and with the chances of us at least getting one each high. This was a small hotel complex called Punta Colorado, on the east-facing shore of the Baja Peninsula in Mexico. Thus was Margherita Tours born. This was the name Rob devised and quoted to me when discussing our impending travel arrangements, as he did much of the organising himself online.

Our research suggested the best time for the striped marlin was the end of April through to June, so we chose the last few days of April and the first days of May, in 2001. This was when the weather seemed to be most predictable too, giving us the best chance of maximising our days at sea.

Just as before, the planning, tackle selection and deselection process, along with more research, was extensive. Between us we put together a small selection of marlin and tuna lures, which I pre-rigged myself. We chose to take most of our own rods and reels, but would rely on the boat tackle for the heavier marlin, purely because of airline luggage hold weight restrictions. We both had USA-made outfitter tackle bags, both stuffed full, the stitching fit to break, but we were confident we had enough tackle, lures and terminal tackle to cover most possibilities. It wasn't just the marlin we would target. We wanted to catch as many species as possible, and would be shore fishing at night too.

The flight was from Heathrow to Houston, USA, then Houston to Cabo Airport in Baja. At the airport we would be picked up by the hotel and driven the hundred or so miles to the accommodation. One slight concern was that we were warned that even in this day and age, road bandits with guns were possible while travelling between the airport and the hotel through remote country. But marlin are marlin, and nothing would put us off. The journey, thankfully, went without mishap and we arrived at the hotel in one piece. You entered through an archway covered in stunning purple bougainvillea. As we checked in at reception, I looked out across the bars patio to the azure blue Sea of Cortez and watched fish breaking in the surf below the hotel.

The next morning, April the 28th, we were picked up on the beach by a small dinghy at 6am, taken out to a waiting bait boat where we purchased live sardines, locally called sardinios, and then boarded the fishing boat. The crew spoke no English, and we little Spanish, but they realised we were Roberto and Miguel. It was likely any other business would be concluded using hand signals and single words. It was thus, the captain said, "Marleen, Señor?", and we replied, "Si, Capitan". We were about to troll for marlin and set a course offshore.

When marlin fishing the captain usually steers from the fly bridge high up above the cabin looking all the time for surface signs of fish. This can be a marlin sat on the surface, tail fin out of the water, maybe frigate birds soaring high but monitoring marlin below that we cannot see, or feeding birds diving in the water, porpoise breaching, or just a change in the sea's surface that creates a wind or current line. Rob and I decided we wanted to be as much part of this day as possible, so we also constantly scanned the horizon.

Three times during the early morning the crew spotted marlin on the surface. The boat would violently turn without warning

Yellowfin Tuna Muppet Rig

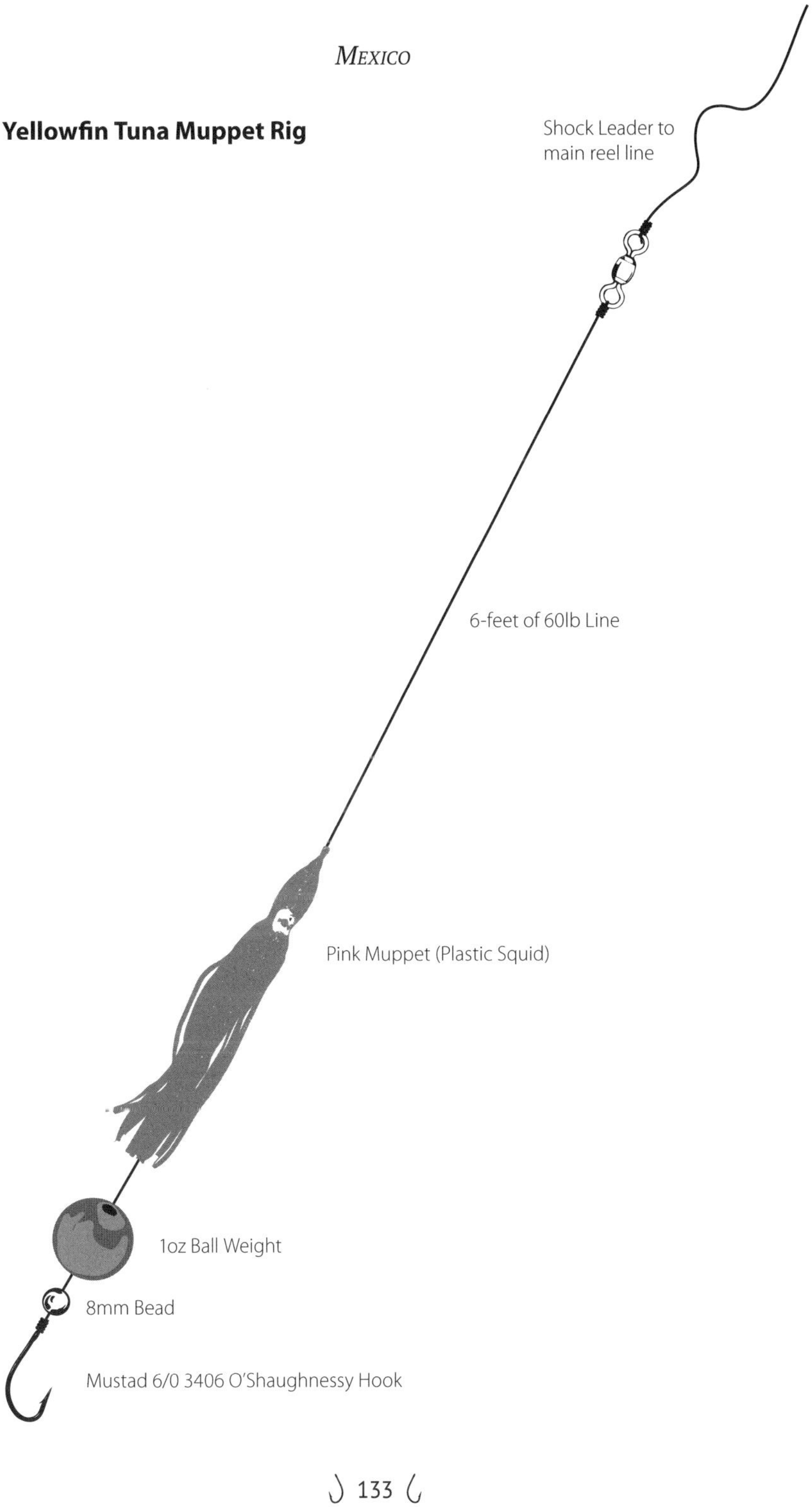

and accelerate towards the fish. The fish would dive. Some then take the lures, some don't. We found the 'don't' kind. It was 11.20 am, the sun warm and firing back off the white deck. The sea was like a mirror. In the distance to the west the dry brown mountains kissed a deep blue, cloudless sky.

Suddenly the boat veered hard to the south, the engine revved and we were moving fast. In the distance we saw a flock of wheeling and diving birds with porpoise breaching and fish scattering on the surface. The boat slowed and the lures worked through the feeding mass, but nothing took. We could see yellowfin tuna breaking surface and I was desperate to catch one. But how?

I had a 20lb class PENN Slammer boat rod with an ABU 7000C reel on, this loaded with just 18lb mono line. I thought quickly what to do. I rapidly fed the line through the rod rings, attached a strong 3/0 swivel, tied on six feet of 60lb line, slid on a four-inch pink muppet (plastic squid), slid on a one-ounce ball-weight, an 8mm bead, and tied on a size 6/0 Mustad O'Shaughnessy hook. The muppet head would sit over the ball-weight and the muppet legs move and shimmer as the lure was pulled along. I threw this over the side, fed about 50 yards of line off the reel and held the rod tip low over the stern to get the muppet a little deeper, with a half way set reel drag. The rod buckled over and a fish ripped line off the reel. It was a 10lb yellowfin tuna, quickly followed by another. Out went the pink muppet a third time, but I let more line off this time to get the lure deeper.

I had to wait no more than 30 seconds, then the rod, without warning, was nearly wrenched from my hands. Whatever ate the lure was now running fast, the reel drag screaming and I feared the reel may not take it. The ABU 7000 is a classic reel, but designed principally for salmon fishing on big rivers, not battling big offshore game fish. The fish kept running and I watched the line lower on the spool until only a third of it was left. I added a little more drag pressure, then pressured the fish as much as the 18lb line would allow. I listened to the line sing as it stretched to near breaking point. The fish still took line. The reel was now down to maybe 20% line capacity. The fish finally stopped, but now sounded deep. I kept maximum pressure on but was not gaining line. The fish started to go round in tight circles. I could feel the pulse of the tail beats through the rod. I was sweating and had to wipe my forehead to stop beads of stinging sweat running in to my eyes.

I gained a little line, then the fish ran again. It went deeper and circled. I gained line back again, then it went deeper. This went on for well over an hour. I was though, now aware the fish was tiring, and upped the pressure a fraction more. I was gaining line steadily now. The fish came up, flashed under the surface, a hint of yellow, white and silver, then it went vertically down at speed taking back another 50 yards of line. I was conscious of sharks in these waters and did not want to lose my prize to a mouth full of teeth. I worked that Slammer rod right in to the butt and forced the fish up quickly. It broke surface at the back of the boat, I led it gently in, then the crewman gaffed the fish in the jaw and the prize was mine. I glanced at the captain who had a smile nearly as wide as my own. I didn't need to say anything, he knew what I wanted to know. He said, "30 kilo, Señor. Gude feeesh!" The crew wanted the tuna, so out of respect to them, it was kept. A 70lb yellowfin on 18lb line was a good way to start the week. The fight had lasted one hour and 50minutes.

The next day we went out on a small boat called a Panga catching bonito to 9lbs on nine-weight fly rods. I also had a small dorado on the fly, and my first ever rooster fish, a 10lber, on a sardine bait. The following day we shore fished and caught snappers, lizard fish, jack crevalle, croakers, and Rob got a guitarfish and a moray eel. The moray was a strange creature. It was aggressive and bared strong teeth to us, but its skin seemed over sized and did not fit the body properly. It was an odd sight to see!

The 2nd of May was a day to savour. We headed out for marlin. Trolling lures, watching the sea surface out to the horizon for fish sign. The Captain spotted a marlin very early on, but it sank out of sight and would not take. Rob and I have a system when fishing somewhere new for something special. We will toss a coin to see who gets the first fish, then whichever rod goes on the second fish it's the angler yet to catch who takes it. After that we stick to our own rods and take our individual chances. We were trolling at about six knots when the starboard outrigger flipped out. It was Rob's privilege to take the first fish. He picked up the rod, sat in the fighting chair, braced himself, and I watched the rod tip pull hard over in to the most satisfying fighting curve. The striped marlin, now angry, leapt clear of the water several times, before sounding deep. It took over an hour for the fish to show at the stern of the boat. The crewman grabbed the bill, released the lure from the mouth, and we watched the fish slide away to fight another day. The crew said "65-70 kilos, Señor". Rob had his marlin!

The pressure was now on for me to get my first striper. On the 3rd of May there was a light breeze from the south, just enough to ripple the water. We were fishing aboard the *Christina* and sailed at 6am. By 7.30 we had chased two surface showing marlin that did not want to eat. I was anxious, and kept glancing at my watch, conscious of precious time slipping away.

The captain said something to crewman, which I did not understand. We motored on. It was 11.20 and the boat came off its course and tracked east, and slowed right down. There were two marlin nearly side by side on the surface, their sickle shaped tails proud and occasionally moving as the fish steadied itself. As the boat approached quietly, they did not flinch, their tails stayed inert as they basked in the warm surface water. The crewman, to my surprise, grabbed a live sardine from the bait well and pitch cast it to towards the marlin and handed me the rod. One fish was uninterested, but the other slid beneath the waves. My eyes were fixed on the sardine and I saw a dark shape appear rear of the sardine, suddenly change colour to vibrant blues and silver, then flash at the sardine, dorsal fin erect, its mouth wide open, bill cutting water...and the sardine disappeared. I was in the chair, the rod buckling over as the marlin put distance between it and me, line zinging off the reel at an amazing rate. I watched the line angle in to the water shallow and said to Rob, "It's coming up, it's going to jump", and as I said that the fish leapt head first and vertical clear of the surface, tail wagging, water streaming off its flanks. It greyhounded away using up three more leaps, then went deeper and ran fast. The speed with which these fish can take line has to be experienced to be believed.

I was sweating now, the fish was deep swinging side to side as it swam, fast in short bursts, then slower and more determined.

I felt the fish coming up in the water. It leapt twice more and I dropped the rod tip to ease the pressure on the hook hold. So many marlin are lost when they leap, often because the hook pulls free under pressure. Rob said "45 minutes", he was timing the fight. The fish was circling at depth and again sharks went through my mind. I pressured the fish, working the rod and line to the maximum. The fish came up gradually, then turned and was coming up fast. It leapt four more times all well clear of the water, and I drew breath again when the line stayed tight and the fish went down deep. That took a lot out of the fish and steady pressure was now telling on her. We saw colour deep down, the flash of blue and silver, the fish swaying her head side to side as she changed direction. The fish was just 20 feet down now, the colours more vivid, the dorsal fin erect and only slightly moving. One last sustained spell of pressure and the fish broke surface. The crewman grabbed the leader and lead the fish to the boat side. He grabbed the bill and held the fish. The captain looked at me. His eyes spoke the question, do we keep the fish or not? I shook my head. We tried to get a photo, but it was more important the fish went back. I made a point of touching the fish, felt the grain of the bill, helped hold the fish while she recovered, then in unison with the crewman we let her slip from our grasp. I watched the fish sink slowly, then her tail wagged and she disappeared gradually in to the deep blue. The crewman shook my hand, then the captain, who said, "75 kilos, Señor!" Rob and I both had our first striped marlin under our belts.

Before the day was out we also saw some debris on the surface and ran lures past it. I caught a 45lb bull dorado and Rob got a female dorado of about 30lbs. We finished the trip the next day aboard a small panga, Rob catching three rooster fish to 20lbs, me getting a 20lb jack crevalle that took an hour to beat on 12lb line. That night, our last in the bar, we set our minds on coming again to fish these magical waters.

BLUE IS THE COLOUR

We were so enamoured with Punta Colorado that we set in motion plans to get back there the very next year immediately we got home. This time though, due to work commitments, we had to go a little later at the beginning of June. 2002 had, so far, proved inconsistent regards the weather inside the Sea of Cortez. It had been windier than usual and not as warm as would be expected, though as we were heading out the weather improved and the temperature rose a little.

Due to the long plane journey and our previous experience we chose not to fish offshore the first day. It was to be a day of relaxing so we were fully prepared for the second day when we'd be chasing roosterfish. However, as is ever the case, we could not resist having a cast having first downed a margarita and a couple of beers. We grabbed spinning rods and went to the right of the hotel to where the rocks stop and the sandy beach begins. Rob went further on than me. I stayed near where the rocks met the beach. I was casting a small 1oz spinner on a light spinning rod and 14lb line. I was catching a few small colorado snappers and croakers and was happy enough. I made a long cast out in to open water, and had only retrieved a few turns when something smashed the spinner, felt the hook, turned for the horizon and burned off a good 50 yards of line on its first run. It paused way out, then went again taking a longer run of maybe 75 yards. It shook its head, thumped around, and sulked. I tried to put some pressure on it, but it swung its head and went off on another long run and was now close to 200 yards away from me. I only had about 50 yards of line left on the reel, so really bullied the fish as best I could. It was reluctant to come towards me, but gradually I retrieved maybe 40 yards of line. The fish made another run, luckily up the beach, but then doubled back. I stayed in contact with the fish, but now it was way out from where I stood and seemed intent on going to my left heading in to what was rough reefy ground.

I had no choice but to follow the fish. I climbed on to the rocks, trying to keep the rod as vertical and as high as I could. The fish was not running now, but doggedly swimming against rod pressure to the left. I suddenly slipped and falling on to sharp rocks gouged my knee resulting in a wide cut that bled really badly. I ignored the pain and kept fighting the fish. It took me a good hundred yards to the left and fought it out in what appeared to be deeper water. I could do little with it except keep the pressure on, pump the fish in bit by bit by lifting the rod and then retrieving line each time I dipped the rod a little. I was gaining on the fish literally an inch or two at a time. It was hot, I was sweating heavily, and my leg was still bleeding. The fish went solid in the water and used its weight to just hang there. Then it turned back and slowly swam to the right. Gradually though, I was gaining a little more line. Over to my right was the reef that jutted out seaward where I'd cut my leg. I tried to select the highest bits of rock to jump on and keep the rod at a full vertical arms length. I got the fish within 30 yards of the clean sand where we started the battle... then I felt the line grate on something and the line broke. That desolate, heavy, pit of the stomach feeling that pervades the body when a good fish is lost flooded through me. Behind me I heard a huge groan. I hadn't known at the time, but turned to see a large crowd of hotel guests that had gathered on the balcony above and were watching the fight as it unfolded, which, I was told later, had lasted one hour and 20 minutes. What was it? My guess would be a big jack crevalle. Having caught quite a few previously, even while fighting it, my feelings were that it was a big jack, a very big jack.

The 7th of June we spent aboard a small panga fishing just offshore near La Ribera. We had problems getting bait and had to settle for overly large whole mullet. These we freelined off the stern of the boat. The fishing was hard. The fish were hitting the baits but missing the hooks. I eventually hooked a decent dorado, but as it leapt clear of the water we saw the hook and bait fly out of the mouth and it was gone.

We caught some small rooster fish, but lost or missed on the strike a lot more. I changed over to a larger hook, trying to make sure the hook point was well clear of the bait. I put on a new mullet and fed this off the stern of the boat about 50 yards and let the current just take it. I was holding the rod all the time, feeding line off through my fingers, but feeling for bites at the same time. I felt the weight of the mullet disappear, but had the bale-arm of the reel open to allow line to spill off. Line started to peel off the spool, but I let the fish run. I let it run maybe 20 yards, then, as the fish slowed, I flipped the bale-arm over and lifted the rod to strike as the line came tight. Some 70 yards or so away, a huge rooster fish leapt six feet clear of the water thrashing its head side to side, and its massive dorsal fin erect and high as it climbed.

Time seemed to slow as it flipped over in mid air and entered the water head first. There was no pause, this fish tore line off the reel and just kept going, broaching twice as it ran. I dropped the angle of the rod and kept heavy strain on, but it was again only 14lb line, so you can only do so much. The fish ran sideways now across the rear of the boat, went deep, then shot back to the left again dragging line off. It was making shorter runs, but would then surprise and just sulk for a few moments before running again. Slowly the fish stopped running fast, but swam more slowly back and forth, occasionally shaking its head and thumping the rod tip. It was in maybe 25 metres of water, but we were still very close to shore. It ran for the sand, but pressure turned it. It then went out to sea and went very deep. Again I turned the fish, and by using those short pumps of the rod, started to gain more line.

I'd been fighting the fish for an hour now. A solid ever present resistance that moved at will using all its power, strength and weight. It crossed my mind that the hook hold might be weak, also that the knots on the 14lb line might be getting over pressured, but these are natural, understandable thoughts that cross an anglers mind during a long fight with a worth adversary. The captain manoeuvred the boat out in to slightly deeper water away from the shore and the fish was now more under the boat, but only for a second or two. It did not like the noise of the boat engine, turned, and made one last powerful run dragging another 25 yards of line off the reel. This sapped the fish of its strength and with reluctance it slowly came towards me. We saw colour, then it broke surface and looked huge. The captain reached over and lifted the fish aboard. The fight lasted one hour and 22 minutes. It weighed 35lbs. Only when you have felt the power of warm climate fish, can you appreciate what a fast metabolism can do and how hard they pull and fight. That was the last fish of the day.

The next day we trolled for marlin. Rob had a strike on a lure, but this turned out to be a massive wahoo weighing somewhere between 80 and 100lbs. This fish smoked the drag on a brand new Daiwa 6/0 Sealine reel loaded with 50lb mono. It was the only fish of the day! The 9th of June we went fly fishing off the shore driving quad bikes that were as much fun as the fishing. As we parked the quads at the top of the beach near where the scrubland started, we could hear the rhythmical *drrrrrr* of hidden rattlesnakes aware of our presence. Our catch were small roosterfsh, snappers, croakers, and I had a 4lb silver perch. We trolled for marlin again on the 10th and 11th, but blanked.

The 12th we were due out on a boat called the *Vodka*, an offshore cruiser with an excellent and very friendly two-man crew. We'd fished with them two days before, and unfortunately they had forgotten their lunch, so we shared ours with them. They were grateful, and this day had come with food prepared by their wives that we could all share as a thank you. Fresh dorado in a special spicy coating that was delicious, and spicy wraps. We had a good rapport with this crew and they tried hard to catch us fish. We trolled far, but nothing was happening. The captain decided to lift the lures and move faster visually looking for marlin on the surface. We saw several, threw live sardine to them, but none were interested. As in previous days, the fishing was very hard. Life in the sea was lethargic and uncaring. We went back to trolling lures. The pattern was a mix of colours, but with the day being bright I'd asked the crewman to run a dark purple lure on the port side, and a long way back to get it deeper.

It would not be long before we had to head back. I glanced at my watch and it was 14.15. As I looked at my watch the outrigger on my side pinged out and a reel started to scream. The boat was mainly equipped with 50lb class tackle, but it was the single 30lb class rod armed with a PENN Senator 4/0 that purred in to life as the marlin ran. I grabbed the rod before the crewman could get there and set the hook. Line poured off the reel non-stop. The fish just kept going. Instead of sitting in the chair I wanted to fight this fish stood up and made it clear to the crew that's what I wanted to do. I felt the fish coming up in the water. Up and up, I knew she would jump, and then far off at the back of the boat this majestic, incredible creature threw its whole body clear of the water, thrashed it tail and head side to side, flipped in mid air and entered the water sideways making a massive explosion of white water. It jump immediately again, then twice more, and sounded. It was a fast moving fish, full of fight and power. Up it came and jumped five times in quick succession, smashing the water to foam. Now it tail wagged across the water maybe 20 feet, then sounded again. It fought deep now for maybe five minutes, then rose to the surface and leapt no less than six times one after the other. It stayed shallow and I briefly saw the bill out of the water thrashing side to side as it tried to shake the hook.

The fish was off again dragging line from the spool, then it went deep, deeper than before, and hung with all its weight against me.. I piled the pressure on the fish and forced it to come upwards. It sulked, then moved off slowly, before rapidly accelerating and breaking through the surface to greyhound three more times. That was the last time it jumped. Now it was just a war of attrition, me pulling hard and the fish doing the same. We saw colour at the back of the boat and the fish came slowly in to view, the dark purple konahead had slid up the trace a little way, but the hook was firmly in the upper jaw. The crewman and captain grabbed the bill and held the fish at the side of the boat. I was shocked when he said, "maybe 120 kilos, a blue marlin, Señor!" Never in my wildest dreams had I expected to catch a blue marlin, yet there she was, right in front of my eyes. Someone tried to get a photo, but I was keen to get the fish returned alive and healthy. A photo, as so often happens when Rob and I fish, is the last thing we worry about. We fish to see the fish swim away. I briefly held the fish by the bill, her head in the water, body supported by the crewman. I felt her stir in to life, and she struggled to be free. We both let go and watched her melt back in to her ocean home.

The next day, again aboard the *Vodka*, we saw a lot of striped marlin on the surface, but as before they would not eat early on. Yet when the sun was high in the sky we both had marlin, fish about 100lbs in weight, one on a Mexican flag yellow and green clone, the other on the same purple konahead I had the blue on the day before. Our last day produced nothing. Our Mexico adventure was over. Both trips will stay etched deeply and forever in my mind. Getting my first marlin was amazing, but to add the blue marlin was, for me, something very special, and one of the highlights of my life.

My next adventure takes us to the Land of Fire...Iceland!

Chapter 13
Iceland

Iceland, called the Land of Fire due to its many active volcanoes and steam vents, has a varied mixture of ground feature. In the southwest it has a lunar landscape, and prior to the moon landings in the late 1960's some of the vehicles used, I'm told, were tested here. You can see why, for it is a rugged, in parts, a desolate terrain, yet with its own beauty. The beaches are blessed with black sand, and many of the rocks formed in small flat wave like flows created as the molten rock slowed as it cooled, then ceased to move forever as a visual testament to the earths furnace like inner core of liquid rock. Yet in the northwest there are high jagged peaked mountains, snow topped, high sea cliffs, wild, remote, and all the better for it. The terrain is suggestive that monsters dwell here. And so they do!

I had a call asking if I was interested in visiting Iceland to look at the sea fishing potential and to compile some magazine features to help advertise the country, and its fishing, to the UK public. Quick to agree, I found out I would be working with Steve Mason. Steve is from the Northeast of England, but had been working in countries all around the world, mainly as a professional fish filleter. It was while working in the north of Iceland, and being a keen and experienced sea angler, that he realised the sea angling potential available on the Icelandic coast, and set up a company to bring anglers in from the UK and Ireland to fish.

My first trip out was to the Reykjavik area in July, 2006. It was a short five-day affair to check out the shore fishing, but saw me catch my first wolfish, a big lemon sole, plus huge numbers of haddock, dabs, whiting and cod, and witness a massive 16lb torsk caught from the shore by Steve. I also fished the fly and took coalfish to 6lbs from both the jetties and the open rock ledges. It was obvious the sea angling potential was huge and it was my hope to return as soon as possible to witness much more of what, at the time, was really a very well kept secret. A couple of other shore trips followed. Talking to Steve he kept telling me of when he worked in the Northwest fjords in an area known as Isafjordur. There were a few German parties travelling to this ground, but again, at the time, little was really known about the areas boat fishing, and next to nothing of the shore fishing. We arranged a trip, and I would be accompanied by magazine editor Barney Wright, my son Mike Jr, and Steve would lead the party.

We met Steve at Reykjavik Airport, and after piling ridiculous amounts of gear and tackle in to Steve's car, we headed north for Bolungarvik in the northwest fjords. I watched the scenery slowly change from the flatter moon like landscape, gradually getting higher and more ice eaten as we progressed north. We arrived to find a strong wind blowing from the north, sometimes switching east, and it looked rough across the fjord.

The following morning was little better. The wind was cold and still strong, but the sky was blue, and when out of the wind the sun offered a little warmth and was comforting. We were scheduled to go out on a boat skippered by a German guy. It turned out he only knew two throttle settings, stop and flat out. The journey out in to the fjord was rough and no amount of chat suggesting he slow down made any difference. It was full throttle all the way. We tried to sit on the deck, as standing was impossible, but were literally bouncing up a good foot or more at times as he charged through every oncoming wave. We were relieved when the boat suddenly came to an abrupt stop. We tried to fish on the drift in the middle of the fjord, but the drift, with the wind, was way to fast. I suggested to Steve, who in turn suggested the same to the skipper, that we try along the inner edge of the south side of the fjord where the wind would be less.

The water here was some 120 feet deep generally, but on the first drifts I noticed, that corresponding with a lift in the land ashore, there was a deeper hole that went down to 190 feet with

Whitby Rig

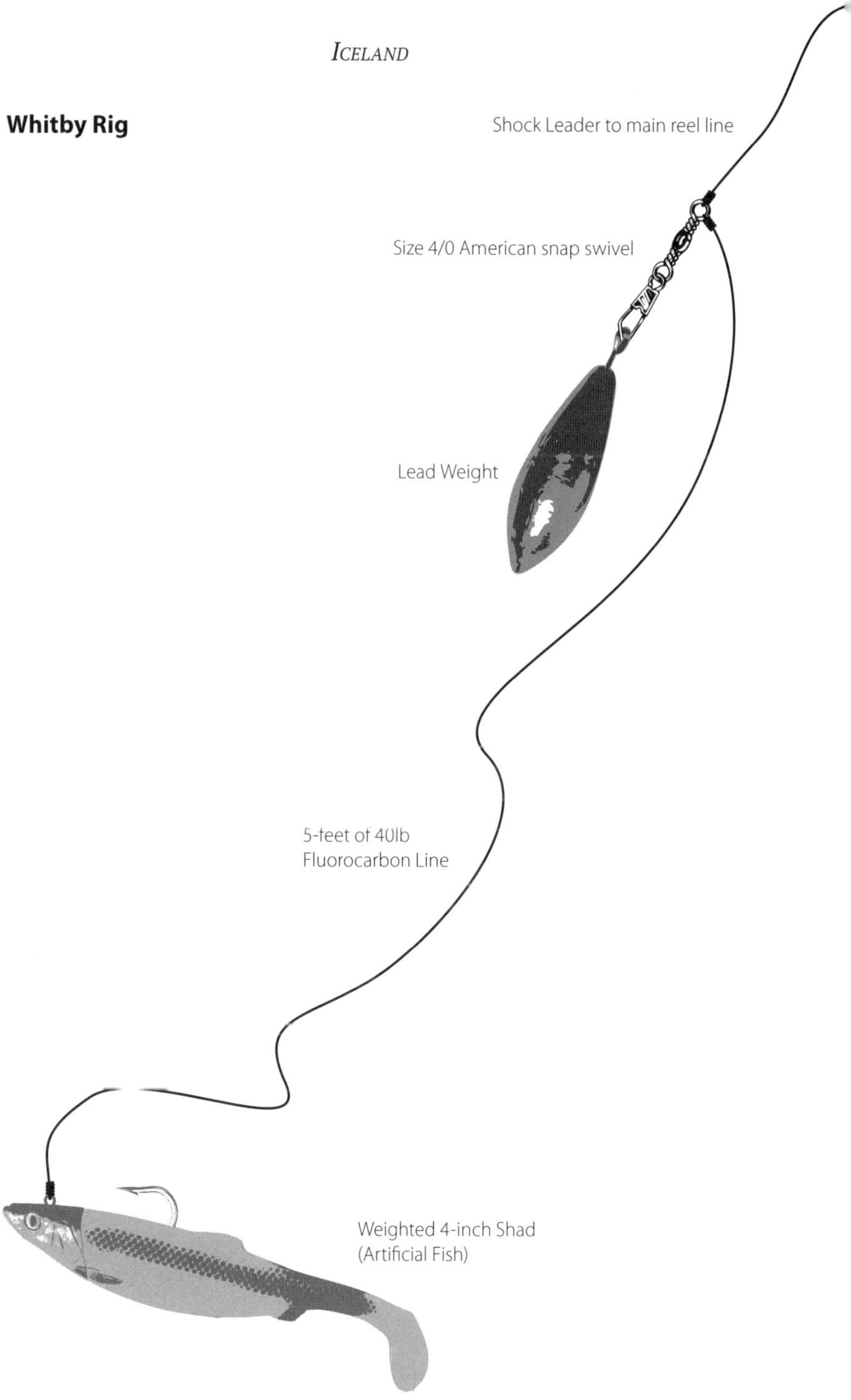
Shock Leader to main reel line
Size 4/0 American snap swivel
Lead Weight
5-feet of 40lb
Fluorocarbon Line
Weighted 4-inch Shad
(Artificial Fish)

a near-vertical ledge on the east side that faced west. We were drifting east to west. I felt there was a chance of bigger fish in the hole, so kept a careful watch as to when we neared the lift on the shore with each drift.

We were using a range of artificial eels and shads. We were catching lots of cod to 12lbs, and the occasional good haddock to 6lbs. I was fishing a weighted four-inch shad simply rigged by tying an American snap swivel to the shock leader, attaching the lead weight to the link clip, then tying on five feet of 40lb Fluorocarbon line to the same eye I'd tied the leader to. This is called the 'Whitby rig', and is simple, non-tangle tackle, but highly effective. I wanted to 'hop' the lure up and down a few feet above the seabed to target the bigger cod I knew would be deep down and working fairly tight in to that vertical ledge. It was essential that I watch the shore lift as an indicator of when we were approaching the wall, and get the lure down quickly to fish the deepest part of the hole at the base of the vertical wall.

As the shore marker came level I dropped the lure down until I felt it hit bottom. Retrieved about eight feet of line, then simply lifted the rod tip up and down using just my wrist to 'hop the lure along. It was only a few seconds before the rod tip slammed over and a fish thumped deep below shaking its head and pulling a few feet of line off the reel. The fish, I knew instantly, was bigger than what we'd previously caught. It came up grudgingly, foot by foot, then wallowed on the surface to be netted by Barney. It weighed 18lbs. The other lads were also in to fish with Mike Jr picking up a 17lber and Barney one about 14lbs. I had time for one more drop on this drift, and bagged another cod about 18lbs. I was watching the shore marker and got down a few seconds earlier on the next drift. Again, as soon as the lure hit the seabed, a fish grabbed it. I had two that drift, one of 21lbs and the second 23lbs. Mike Jr got a 21lber and Barney and Steve both had fish about 18lbs.

The wind was increasing and it was not easy fishing. The next drift I got the timing exactly right and the lure was straight down the front of the vertical wall. I felt it tap bottom, lifted it, then hopped it along. The rod tip bumped, then pulled right over tensing the rod right down in to the upper butt. This fish stayed deep, shook its head and was reluctant to come up. It fought using head down lunges taking a few feet of line, then one steady longer run for the bottom that took maybe 15 yards of line off the reel. It was my best yet at 26lbs.

The next drift, again I got the shad right down the side of the wall. I immediately started to work it, and what I can only describe as a steam train hit the lure in one solid thump. There was a brief pause, then the rod tensed over and a great weight shook its head as cod do, then pulled line off the reel. This felt a big fish and I played it with consistent pressure, but also with great care. It was not a fish I was willing to lose. The fish was heavy, kept turning towards the bottom taking a few feet of line, then lunge and circle, then try for the bottom again. It was still deep and I felt its head shake three times side to side trying to rid itself of the shad in its jaw. Slowly I worked the fish upwards. Steve was fishing alongside me and he saw the faint dull white of the fish deep down in the crystal clear water. You could see it twist and turn, go in circles, then twist and turn some more. It broke surface. This cod had a really deep rounded belly, was heavy and thick behind the head, and Barney and Steve lifted it aboard for me. At the time it was the biggest cod I'd ever seen and weighed a little over 37lbs when we got ashore. We only had one more drift over that ground in rapidly worsening weather, but I added another 26lb cod with the lads getting cod in the high teens, the best another 19lber for Mike Jr.

I felt if we could have fished on over this mark a 40lb cod would have been caught, and possibly even a 50lber. The big cod were in numbers there and eager to feed. Fishing though, is often like that. You get a taste of what might be possible, but fate intervenes and you don't quite get all of what might have been. No matter. It was an incredible run of fish, even for Iceland, in just a few short drifts.

We had a couple more days at sea, again in bad weather, but nothing to equal the fishing of the first day, though some good wolfish and torsk where taken, more cod, and nice haddock over 6lbs. We returned one night and as we docked, some commercial fisherman had tipped opened shells down the side of the pier. Looking over the side there was a cloud of literally hundreds of big dabs swimming over the carpet of shells. It was a sight none of us will ever forget and it now proves to me as a timely reminder of how here in the UK we have squandered once massive stocks of fish.

I was back shore fishing in Iceland in July of 2010. I was able to take a friend with me, Francis Jones from Abertillery, South Wales. Francis is a Welsh shore international angler with vast experience. We were also to be joined by John McInnes, a Scottish angler and ex tank crew, again with Steve Mason leading the party. We flew in to Reykjavik and headed north, this time for Dalvik and Olafsfjordur. This is an impressive fjord surrounded by mountains, and while fishing I imagined a tough no-nonsense Viking called Olaf sailing his Viking long ship up this fjord to settle here and give the district its name.

The first day we caught cod, dabs, coalfish, and I got a small halibut off the shore at Haugnes. The second day we fished Pier 200 in Dalvik. In less than five hours fishing the four us estimated conservatively that we caught over 650lbs of fish including cod, haddock and dabs. Trying to avoid the smaller cod up to 7lbs, I was fishing a whole bluey body (bluey being a garfish shaped Pacific saury fish imported in to Iceland for commercial fishing bait) with the head and tail chopped off, this being about ten inches long. It got me the biggest cod of the day at a little over 11lbs, and I had a Arctic starry ray, another new species for me. The numbers of fish in front of us that day was staggering, and all of them were released. If we'd fished another three hours, without doubt we would have exceeded 1000lbs of fish in under eight hours of fishing.

The next day, we fished a commercial pier in the little town of Olafsfjordur. On the left side of the pier was the entrance to a deep water harbour, and Francis had a plaice out of here first cast. Steve and John fished the middle and end of the pier, and I fished the right-hand side where a big wall ran all the way to the end of the pier. It was difficult to cast from with the wall in the way, but I managed by casting high over the wall, then pulling the rod to the left with the lead weight still flying through the air. I caught a cod of 7lbs first cast, followed by several more, in addition to a couple of good dabs. What I always try to do when fishing somewhere new is to spread my casts around dropping some in short and others long in a basic fan shape. This allows me to cover more ground and pick up little features that may be on the seabed. I'm looking for deeper holes, little patches of stone, weed beds and the like. Specific feature that might hold fish!

While fishing the Olafsfjordur pier, and casting to different areas, I found a small patch of rough ground out to my right at about 80 yards. The surrounding ground was quite clean being mostly muddy sand. I decided to concentrate on this patch of stone and kept putting baits on to it. I began by catching cod up to 6lbs, but then hit a fish that fought differently. I figured correctly it was a haddock, and landed a cracking looking haddock of 4lbs 8ozs. Even in Iceland a haddock over 4lbs off the shore is a very good fish. Over the next three hours I kept hitting a mix of cod, whiting, dabs, but also haddock. One after another the haddock took the bait and ended up catching seven haddock over 4lbs, these being 4lb 3ozs, 4lb 6ozs, 4lb 8ozs, two of 4lb 9ozs, 4lbs 13ozs and the best at 4lbs 15ozs. John also got a cracking fish close to 5lbs as well. It was shore fishing for haddock at its best. That same mark also saw me catch my first ever long rough dab. It had been a special day!

That night, after seeing me fish hard for a few days, as everyone did, but also run around all day with the camera taking literally well over 100 photos per day, and take the necessary notes for the forthcoming features, Francis said to me, "Do we get a rest at all and a decent nights sleep?" I replied, "No! We keep going until we go home." He said, "I thought your job was easy, but its damn hard work, and I don't know how you do it without a break." I guess you get used to it; angling journalism, if you are full-time, is hard work, and not what people envisage it to be at all. But I'm not complaining, just stating a fact that Francis rightly picked up on.

I always take a fly rod with me on my trips. I target both coalfish and cod on the fly, and its great fun. Without the added weight of a lead weight, the fish can fight to their full capacity. But you need to target them in different ways. I make my own flies. They do not need to be big, but you need to get them down in the water quite quickly. I tie them, with a weighted eye, but dress them quite thinly and use maribou as it looks so alive in the water and will pulse and shimmer as you retrieve the fly. For coalfish, good colours are red and white and black as the coalfish will look for and attack a distinct silhouette. For cod I like all white with some silver in it, yellow and white, or a fly with pink in it. The coalfish are generally up in the water and tend to be around the base of jetty supports or down the side of stone made breakwaters. The cod are much deeper and are working at seabed level. When casting I cast as far as possible, then release line until I feel the lure is on the seabed. For cod I use short, slow pulls taking in no more than six inches of line at a time. I aim to keep the fly near the seabed as long as possible, but then as it starts to rise keep the ascent as slow as possible. This works and will take any cod that follow the fly without eating it just as the fly starts to climb. For coalfish, I strip the fly in quickly using double pulls, but also let the fly sink momentarily before resuming the retrieve. As the fly starts to climb I retrieve even faster as the coalfish will then attack the fly thinking it is about to get away.

We fished Haugnes Pier again the following night. The other lads fished baits and spinners catching cod and coalies, John getting a cracking coalie of 8lbs 12ozs on a spinner. I fished the fly and started to initially target the cod. I had several, the best about 3lbs. I then changed to a bigger but lighter fly and went for the coalfish. I was casting along the length of the pier, letting lots of line out, then stripping fast as the fly started to come up off the seabed. I hit coalies straight away taking several fish to 4lbs. The depth off the end of the pier was about 25 to 30 feet. I went within casting range of the end of the pier. Cast out, then let the fly sink much longer. As I started to retrieve I'd only made a few pulls, when something grabbed the fly, turned for the jetty supports and ripped line off the reel, me trying to add extra drag by putting the flats of my inner fingers on the rim of the spool. The fish was powerful and fought hard, but luckily came out from under the pier and bored off out in to deeper water away towards a small harbour. The fish was running at will, but slowly tiring. Steve netted it for me and we weighed it prior to release at 5lb 6ozs. I had a couple more fish in the 4lb range, then hit another bigger fish. This took the fly, felt the hook, then went straight out to sea towards a breakwater and I just managed to turn it by dropping the rod to my right side and applying maximum pressure. This fish then turned and charged back towards me. I had to manually strip back line to keep pace with the speed of the fish, even then it had some slack. This fish went deep and hung there, made one last run, then fought slowly to the surface where again Steve netted it. This one weighed 5lbs 13ozs. Great fun on a fly rod off the shore!

I was back in Olafsfjordur with Steve Mason and my fishing buddy Colin Albert, also Joe MacDonald, a friend of Steve's, in August, 2012. There is a ferry leaves Olafsfjordur for Grimsey Island, this being Iceland's most northerly territory some 25 miles north of the mainland with nothing between it and the ice cap. The island covers only two square miles, has only one settlement called Sandvik, and has mostly less than 90 inhabitants. The Arctic Circle dissects the island across its northern half. It is famous for the number of birds, also for whale watching. Steve had long wanted to fish here, and so did I. We had just three days to find out what we could about the potential for rod and line fishing off the Grimsey shore.

The island has, for the most part, high inaccessible cliffs on the north side, but is flatter with easier sea level access facing south, and in some parts to the west. There is also a commercial pier where the ferry and working boats land that gives access to deepish water. We fished the rock ledges in the southwest corner the first two days taking cod to 6lbs on bluey baits. At night we fished the pier and enjoyed great fishing, though the cod were smaller fish to 7lbs, these taken on baits and on spinners. Colin had a superb coalfish weighing 18lbs 8oz on bait to prove what could be caught there. I also had cod and coalfish to 4lbs on the fly. The last day we again had just four hours to fish before catching the ferry back for the mainland. Using spinning tackle armed with spinners and weighted shads, we caught a huge number of cod, the best 9lbs. I also had a coalfish of 7lbs 10ozs.

I changed over to the fly rod, unable to resist one last go on the light tackle. I hooked a succession of coalfish, including one that took over five minutes to beat and weighed 5lbs 10ozs. I then switched to heavier lead-headed flies and went for the cod. It was a fish a cast. Often, just as I worked the fly along the seabed after just two or three pulls the tip would dip, the middle of the blank tense, and the reel would sing as it gave line as a fish bored off across the seabed, shaking its head and hugging the bottom. My best cod on the fly weighed 6lbs 5ozs and again took over five minutes to land in the deeper water where it could use all its weight against the light rod. I fished one hour and 50 minutes with the fly rod and counted the cod I caught at 23. I was making my last few casts, and had in fact, packed the rest of my gear, as the others lads were also packing up. I made a long cast straight out, let the heavy cored line sink, while at the same time feeding line off the reel so that I did not lose any distance. I felt the line settle on the seabed, then began twitching the fly back. This time, somewhat surprisingly, the fly was left alone. No fish were interested. I kept the fly coming and felt the line start to rise and lift the fly with it. The line was now vertical in front of me hanging straight down from the fly rod. As I pulled the fly upwards the last few feet I saw colour behind the fly. The colour grew in size. It then materialised in to a cod, dusky bronze on the back, mottled in brown coloured blotches on the flanks, with a big head and its mouth wide open literally a few inches now behind the fly. The cod was big, much bigger than anything we'd so far had on the baits. I looked in to the cod's eye, still having the presence of mind to keep the fly coming to imitate a natural presentation. The cod looked at me, mouth still agape, pelvic fins moving just enough to keep it balanced, still pondering whether to take the fly. My heart was in my mouth, my head inwardly screaming, "Take it, take it", but it didn't. The fish, without a flicker of the tail or a fin, simply sank slowly out of sight and was gone. How big? Certainly between 15lbs and 20lbs. The fish of a lifetime on a fly rod from the shore, but for some reason, it changed its mind. I tried a few more casts, literally with the ferry now in view, but it was pointless and the chance was gone. I still see that fish in my minds eye. What a fight that would have been! It was not to be.

The northwest and north coast of Iceland holds massive potential. You do feel sometimes, that the numbers of smaller fish literally off the shore are so great, that it is percentage fishing. You need to keep catching the smaller fish to increase your chances of a double figure cod. It is a war of attrition, simply the more cod you catch, the more likely you are to hook a big one. That day on the boat off Bolungarvik when I caught several 20lb-plus cod including the 37lber, illustrates just what is available off this amazing coast. That day we were little more than a quarter of a mile offshore. If there were more anglers fishing this Icelandic northwest and north coast, the big fish hotspots would quickly be found. As it is this is virgin fishing, and I'd argue all the better for it. Fish of 20lbs and 30lbs , maybe even 40 or 50lbs will be caught from the shore here, but the lack of rod and line pressure means it will take time to prove the consistency of the fishing. I also feel there are big halibut here to be caught off the shore too. Time will tell, but sooner or later, Iceland will make the news just like Norway has.

And that leads me perfectly in to heading east to the deep, clear waters of the Norwegian fjords and the secrets those mystical waters hold.

Chapter 14
Norway

Though the fishing is the most important part, for me good scenery, especially mountain scenery, is the icing on the cake. Norway is just such a place. The deep fjords with high rising sides and a backdrop of snow topped mountains is such a perfect place to fish. I always find time to take in this scenery, breath in the fresh unpolluted air, and savour special moments watching fish eagles hunt, whales breaching, and wildlife on the shoreline going about their daily chores. It is a true sense of freedom. A million miles away from the frantic battle that encompasses so many modern lives. I fell in love with Norway as soon as my feet touched her hallowed ground.

I was writing for *Total Sea Fishing Magazine* and was contacted by the editor, Barney Wright, asking if I would accompany him to compile some features in Norway. We would be guided by Ian Peacock. Ian is from the Northeast of England, brought up on the rock scars where every cod caught is hard fished for. He was working for a Norwegian Angling Holiday company organising holidays for UK anglers in Norway, and having fished extensively there, no one knew the Norwegian hotspots better than Ian.

We flew out on the 22nd July, 2007. Our fishing destination was Senja, the second largest island in Norway, not counting Svalbard. It is connected to the mainland via the Gisund Bridge. Senja is said to be 'Norway in miniature' due to its diverse scenery, with the western and northern coasts comprised of steep mountains and cliffs rising sheer from the sea, but the south and east of the island being less exposed with a milder climate, seeing forests, rivers and agricultural land.

Our log cabin accommodation looked out on to the fjord. The early morning light cast deep shadows across the mountain sides creating illusions of faces, and this is the land of the Trolls allowing your imagination to run riot. Late in the evening as the sun dipped on to the horizon, the mountains were bathed in a purple ultra-violet light that gave the scenery a cocktail of colour.

We found ourselves sharing the accommodation with a party of German anglers. These included Volker Dapoz, who designed and manufactured the now famous Seawaver Giant Jigheads, a lure that was, in the future, to catch me some of my best Norwegian fish. It was a good group that would talk long in to the night about fish, fishing and life. We alternated breakfast duties too, the Germans providing cheese and German sausage one day, the next we would all eat English fair of bacon, eggs, beans and toast.

The fishing was good, but not easy. We explored some ground towards Kuengr out to the west, also the next fjord to the south initially catching numbers of cod to 12lbs, redfish, whiting, ling, torsk and coalfish. Most of these were on metal pirks and speed jigs, though I did well using weighted rubber shads fished on short booms.

We had noticed that at night, though the sun barely sets, as the light levels drop, the big coalfish resident in the deep fjords rise up in the water column and will harass smaller coalfish on the surface. We decided to target these with metal speed jigs and pirks, though I had designs on also catching them on the fly.

Prior to coming out to Senja, I was lucky enough to be able to get some special ten-weight fly lines made for me with an ultra heavy core. These, I knew, would be awful to cast due to their heavy nature making it difficult to fully aerialize them, but my intention was to get as much line cast out as possible, then feed line off the reel to get the line, and fly, down to maximum depth. It was not much of a problem if the line ended up fishing vertical. What was a concern was if there was a strong breeze that pushed the boat along too fast. This would result in the fly line being towed and bringing it too near the surface to be fully effective for the bigger coalfish feeding deeper under the smaller ones. I'd also made some special flies. These were not overly big, only a couple of inches long, but I'd added two sets of metal eyes to the fly to give it some extra weight to help it get down deep in the water. I'd also made up some flies with small artificial squid bodies with plastic legs and marabou tails as an alternative.

The night of the 26th July was nearly flat calm. We headed north to Torskenfjorden. It was late at night, but the sun, now low in the sky, lit the mountains to the north in a golden hue. I watched cloud spill downwards from a cliff top in a huge wave like a giant waterfall, before it hit warmer air below and stayed, held in suspension, as a clear demarcation line. The sea was oily flat, the reflection of the mountains almost mirror perfect, only disturbed by the occasional settling of a seagull or baitfish breaking surface.

We began fishing the bottom catching cod, ling, torsk and I had a 7lb haddock. As we drifted along, it was now well past 10pm. Suddenly the surface of the fjord erupted in patches of feeding coalfish, slashing across the water with smaller bodies hurling themselves fully airborne trying to avoid the death trap jaws below. Barney and Ian fished the pirks and immediately hit coalfish to 10lbs, but these were deeper than anticipated at about 90 feet. I caught a few, including one of 14lbs, then decided enough was enough. It was time to pick up the fly rod.

I got as much fly line airborne as possible, and shot as much line as I could to maximise the casting distance. The heavy line sank quickly and I stripped line off the reel to maintain both depth and distance. I fed off all the fly line, and about 20 to 30 yards of braid backing. I then started to strip the fly in fast. Immediately I was in to coalfish up to 4lbs, that in the deep water fought for every inch of depth. On a new cast, as I started to strip line, a fish took the fly. I was anticipating the typical vertical crash dive of a coalfish, yet it did not happen. This fish thumped the rod tip, tried to dive using jagged head shakes, then started to swim in tight circles, before lunging for the seabed again. I slowly fought the fish to the surface. When it showed as it rolled on its side close to the boat, we were all stunned. We were fishing in a depth of about 460 feet, but with the fly hooked neatly in the scissors of the jaw, there lay a haddock. It weighed 4lbs 11ozs. Haddock are normally a ground living fish seeking out an existence within a few feet of the seabed, but here in the deeps fjords of Norway, they seem happy to rise in the water column and take advantage of the feed available right at the surface. This turned out not to be a fluke either, as during the evening I had two more haddock on the fly. One close to 4lbs and another just over. I doubt there are many anglers lucky enough to have caught haddock on the fly. It is a rare occurrence, though in Norway, anything is possible!

As the light faded even more, the coalfish went cannibal smashing small coalfish on the surface. In amongst the coalfish were herring, and we could see the oil slicks left by those already eaten on the surface mixed with floating scales. I continued to work the fly hitting coalfish after coalfish. I found that although the smaller fish would take a fast retrieved fly, the bigger fish wanted an ultra fast retrieve. I had to hold the rod under my arm, and strip the line back using both hands. The fly would come easily, then stop dead, a brief pause ensued, then the fish, realising it was hooked , crash dived for the seabed. It was exhilarating fun. I had several fish around the 6lb mark, then hit a better fish that took a lot of line off the reel on its first dive, then went deeper with the second. I had to keep full pressure on the fish working the fly rod to its maximum. The fight lasted close to ten minutes and proved to be an 8lb coalfish. If you think an 8lb coalfish is easy on a ten-weight fly outfit, then you need to rethink. Your arm aches all the way to the shoulder as you work the fish up from depth, your shoulders ache, and its a real relief when the fish comes to the boat. All that taken in to consideration, it is the very best way to target these fish for maximum sport and fun.

For the last two days the weather turned rough. The long fjords always give you some shelter and we continued to catch cod to nearly 20lbs, haddock, torsk, redfish, whiting, ling, and Ian got a 10lb angler fish on a pirk. I photographed this fish and was amazed to see its eye constantly changing colour, going through shades of green, yellow and amber. Its man trap jaws agape and full of teeth, and we marvelled at the little 'fishing rod and lure' it gets its name from that adorns its head to entice prey in close. It swam off strongly when we released it.

LUCKY LOPPA

I was back in Norway the following April, this time to fish the Loppa area. We knew there was great fishing here, but at this time the area was relatively new regarding tourism for anglers, so to some extent, we would be fishing experimentally to help fully assess the area. Again we were there to get magazine features and I would be working with *Total Sea Fishing* magazine editor Barney Wright, sub editor Roger Mortimore, with Ian Peacock again coordinating the trip.

As is so often the case in Norway, there was great fishing just out from the pontoon in front of the house in the village of Tverfjord. The first day, the 27th April, Barney and I went exploring the immediate area finding shallow patches just a few feet deep, but also much deeper water towards where the fjord split going west and north with a small island called Klubbhl in the centre. I caught a cod of 17lbs on a big shad fished on a jighead, and we had numbers of cod to 9lbs, torsk, wolfish and haddock. I had a wolfish that was over 10lbs. These are armed with formidable teeth and powerful jaws with a head that looks prehistoric. We also tried ground to the north close to where some commercial long-lines were set, and though there were cod to double figures, for some reason it did not fish that well there.

The next two days, again the wind was too strong from the west to go for Loppa Island, so we spent the time fishing ground inside Langfjord and an area called Sloppegr. We found a pinnacle here that came up from some 90 metres to within 20 metres of the surface. We caught cod to 15lbs and coalfish on this, then swapped over to the fly rods taking cod to 5lbs, and Barney got a redfish on the fly. That night we were all hoping that the wind would drop and we could push further west in to ground we knew held some much bigger fish.

The Norse Gods smiled. The following morning dawned with just a light breeze from the southwest and the rough, white topped sea, bar some ground swell, had eased away. The forecast was good, and the sea would flatten further during the day. We went out westwards through Southbergsfjord, two boats, one astern of the other, with much hope and anticipation of what might be. We passed through the shallow sound at Skatsnaset between Marehl

Island, then west again through Kalvsundet Sound in to the open sea beyond Loppa. We'd decided the best plan was to split up. Each boat to do their own thing. This meant we could experiment and assess as much ground as possible.

Ian and Roger went southwest and west of Loppa Island, we went to the northwest corner of the island and found some ground that came up in several fang shaped peaks from 100 metres to 34 metres. We caught cod to 15lbs here in huge numbers fishing shads and jigheads, and I had a 14lb coalfish. We found the concentrations of fish were between 40 meters and 60 metres deep. The peak furthest north fished the best with Barney enjoying a good scrap with a 21b cod, and we were picking up some double figure coalfish too. Given the fishing seemed to be getting better to the north we decided to head across to the northern end of the island.

Here we found some flatter ground that looks step like, this falling from 20 metres in to 120 metres in a steady fall. I was fishing a 300g Seawaver Giant Jighead with a ten-inch black shad attached over a flat ledge in about 60 metres of water. I was working the lure about ten feet off the bottom with just an easy wrist action to create that deadly hopping motion to the lure. There was no warning when the rod just crashed over and whatever was down there powered back to the seabed. It hung on the bottom for a moment, then took off across the seabed. I was unsure what it was. It did not feel like a cod, and certainly it was not a coalfish, but it had real power. It went through my mind that it might be a halibut, but that was just a guess as I'd never caught one before. I worked the fish up off the bottom. It came steadily, bit by bit, but swam in tight circles, as many fish do. I figured the fish was about half way up, it just went solid briefly refusing to budge, then the fish turned for the seabed and took line off the reel pretty much until it got back close to the seabed in a crash dive. I began the fight all over again. It was bit by bit, and I was fishing a 20/40lb rod with a reel loaded with 30lb braid, so I could apply a fair bit of pressure. The fish was still about 20 metres deep and Barney could see the first inkling of the fishes colour but not confirm what it was. It dived once more taking 15 yards of line, then went to swimming in circles again. Gradually I was gaining line, then I saw the fish before Barney and yelled, "It's a halibut!". The fish broke surface, and what a majestic sight it was. My first ever halibut. Not a huge fish, it went between 25lbs and 30lbs, but it meant a lot as it was another fish I'd dreamed of catching since a boy.

The next day the weather was flat calm, and without a second thought, our intention was to head back to the west side of Loppa Island. Ian and Roger went out further to the north west and had a great day catching cod with many fish in the 20lb class, and big coalies and haddock. Barney and I stayed with the ground where we had the halibut and caught two more, but only small fish to about 8lbs. We also had some incredible numbers of cod, with Barney getting a 18lb fish, and I had one of 21lbs, and a 26lb cod, this on the black shad and 300g jighead combination. We also caught torsk, and wolfish to close on 10lbs.

The 3rd of May would prove to be our last west of Loppa. Barney and I headed to the north end of the island on some new ground we'd identified on the chart. Ian and Roger went further north again out in to deep water. The lads had a great day catching numbers of cod in the 20lb-plus class, and Roger had cod of 31lbs and 35lbs: tremendous fish. The action was so intense and unforgiving that they coined the phrase the 'Loppa gymnasium', a reference to the constant effort of hooking, playing and landing big fish. It was not an exaggeration!

We, on our new ground, found a rock plateau that shallowed at about 35 metres, gradually falling across undulating ground in to 70 meters, then it dropped very quickly in to 320 metres. The fish were concentrated amongst little peaks on the 35 metres to 70 metres plateau. We were in to cod instantly, and there were hardly any under 12lbs, most in the high teens. Both Barney and I both caught fish in the 20lb-plus category, then Barney hit a fish that he initially struggled to hold. After a long fight with the fish boring for the bottom a couple of times, it broke surface and I gilled the fish to lift it aboard. We weighed it at 31lbs, and our best yet.

I'd been fishing a white shad on a jighead, but now changed back to a big black Twister type worm with a big tail. This instantly improved my catch rate and it was fish on as soon as the lure touched the seabed. The fish were so thickly shoaled here that we could feel the jigheads bouncing off them on the way down, something Ian and Roger also commented on. I was working the lure just on the edge of a drop-off when something smashed the lure and dragged line off the reel. This was a steady fight, the fish hanging in the water, but head shaking and making short dives. This proved to be my biggest cod so far, a 27lber. The next few drops produced cod to 20lbs for me, then as my lure was on its way down I glanced at the echo sounder and saw we were about to come over a small peak. I felt the lure hit the seabed, lifted it 10 feet up and worked the lure. Less than a minute later the rod was nearly wrenched from my arms as something big, heavy and stubborn ate my lure. The rod pulled over and I felt the power of the lower mid section and butt tense up to the weight of the fish. It stayed deep, shook its head, took a small amount of line off the reel, then hugged the bottom. I said to Barney, "This is a biggie!" The fish came up about 25 feet, then took the same amount of line back. I fought it upwards, but it turned and the reel grudgingly gave line again. This is how it was for over five minutes. In mid water the fish used its weight just to hang there and used small undulating turns that I felt through the rod. Pressure told and it came up some more. It made another half-hearted dive, but I could feel it was starting to weaken. Barney saw the first colour of the fish at about 15 metres down. As it came closer it looked huge. Just 20 feet down we were wondering if it would be that coveted 40lber. As it broke surface we saw its bulging belly and the heavy weight behind the head, its mouth open and gills flaring. We lifted the fish aboard. It looked massive. Back ashore some four hours later, the fish weighed 38lbs and may well have been a 40lber when first caught as fish can lose a lot of weight and fluid after capture, and this one did lose a lot of fluid while it lay in the fish box. It was a personal best cod for me and illustrates the quality of the fishing found off Loppa Island.

The last three days we spent inside the shelter of the inner fjords as the wind picked up to near gale-force. We were just getting to grips with what Loppa Island had to offer, learning the ground, and how to fish it. I feel, if we'd had the weather for those last three days, we would have easily beaten the 38lber with a much bigger fish. We contented ourselves with consistent catches of haddock, cod, wolfish, torsk and coalfish, but our hearts and minds were still west of Loppa.

HAVOYSUND

I'd been working as a product development consultant to the Pure Fishing Company, and was working on the famous PENN brand. As a result of this, I was invited to fish the PENN Cup and represent the UK, along with UK colleagues Andy Williams, and James Robbins, the Shakespeare brand manager, also Gerry Foote, a tackle dealer from Morecambe, England and England international Alan Yates from Kent. The event was to be fished mainly by people from all over Europe who were either working for PENN, or whom had a connection with PENN via the fishing industry. We were to fish in Havoysund situated in the far north of Norway. Havoysund is a small island, separated from the mainland by the Havoysund Bridge. The sound is narrow, just a couple of hundred metres or so in width in places, but deep. There is next to nothing between Havoysund and the Arctic ice cap. It is remote, yet beautiful.

We arrived on the 2nd July, 2010. The weather forecast for the six days we were there was set to be good, with mainly light winds and a calm sea. At the greeting, we were told that one person from each of the six four man teams would be designated as boat captain and stay with the boat for the duration of the competition. The other anglers were to swap boats twice a day for the four days of competition, which were two slots of three hours per day. The rest of the time, if you had the stamina, you could take the boats out for some private fishing. Having owned and run boats for most of my life, I was asked to take charge of one boat, so would be responsible for the competitors onboard, and to find them some fish. The way the competition worked was on points, and it was obvious that to win the event, you would have to target mainly smaller coalfish. Some competitors wanted to win and go for the small coalies. Others wanted to make the most of fishing in the north of Norway and target some big fish ignoring the competition completely. I decided to see who I had on board and what they wanted to do. If most wanted to fish the competition, that's what we'd do, but if it was a mix of wishes, then I would spend half the time fishing for coalfish, the other targeting the bigger cod and halibut. I thought this the fairest way of all and hopefully would keep the peace.

I took charge of my boat and moored her just on the outskirts of the settlement below our accommodation. I checked her over, made sure I was happy with everything, reset the fish finder to English, then took the charts detailing the ground in the area with me and poured over them trying to identify areas that might produce fish. I could see areas to the north a few miles away that had rising peaks coming up to within 20 meters of the surface. This was prime ground. I also noticed flat shallow ledges to the west that I figured would produce a few halibut. These would be the areas I'd concentrate on. I was expecting the smaller coalfish to be right over the top of the peak ground, with the better halibut and cod on the inclines to the side.

The first night, some others and I, walked down on to a gutting shed jetty adjacent to the boat and fished with spinning gear. I'd been casting a chrome spinner way out in to the channel catching coalfish and cod to 4lbs. On one retrieve I hit a fish that hugged the bottom and would not lift in the water. Luckily the ground feature was fairly clean with just a few rocks and patches of weed. I played the fish hard, which fought like a demon on the light tackle, but still it would not come up in the water. The fish was powerful and I had to walk off the jetty and down on to the boat pontoon to try and land it. James had walked with me and had grabbed the landing net from the boat. I was on the end of the pontoon, the fish still deep down, but tiring. I was putting as much pressure as possible on the fish but did not yet know what it was. It came slowly in to view as it reluctantly came towards the surface. I suddenly realised it was a halibut about 5lbs. James was literally just about to net it when, with the fish now inches away from the safety of the mesh, the fish made one last dive and the hook pulled free, the spinner flying too close for comfort past my head. It was an interesting way to start the week!

For the anglers keen on amassing competition points, luckily the smaller coalfish, running to about 4lbs, were in good number, and as predicted, were shoaling tight right over the top of the rock pinnacles. They were easy to catch too. It was just a case of letting those seeking points fish while we drifted over the peaks, then get the big lures down in the deeper water to find the cod and halibut.

This was the first time, when in Norway, I'd been able to work the boat fully on my own and use my discretion to try and learn more about where the fish were concentrated and feeding. The very first day, deciding to try one of the flat ledges in shallow water, one of the German anglers caught a 20lb halibut, which is what he wanted to catch. We also lost another fish I felt was a halibut when the hook came out early in the fight. In the afternoon competition period I turned my attention to the peaks on the ground in deeper water to the north.

These peaks were all very similar in shape. They came up from a depth of around 100 metres to within 24 metres of the surface. They were often rounded in shape on the tops, with a steady and even incline downwards. However, many of them on the east side had a definite dip or hollow in them. What I found during the competition periods, but also at night when as a UK crew we went out to fish just for fun, was that the best of the cod fishing was always between 20 metres and 70 metres. Below this you were less likely to catch with only the odd cod taken. What I also found was that there was a very good chance that a halibut would be in the hollow or dip as the incline of the bank started to fall way. I was handling the boat, but also fishing myself as we drifted along. I was fishing only for the halibut and was using my favourite giant jigheads with big 10-inch and 12-inch rubber shads. The first night I got a 15lb halibut, and the second day in the afternoon added another 20lb halibut. The third day I went back in the morning competition session to fish the shallow ground off Nipa, and one of the anglers caught another halibut of 22lbs, followed that night when fun fishing with James Robbins getting a 25lb halibut in just 22 metres of water on a rubber shad.

On the fourth day I pushed out on to some new ground slightly more to the west to some other peaks. These fished extremely well and the lads with me caught three more halibut, and located some good cod, a couple over 20lbs including a 23lb fish. We went back as a UK collective the following night. I had James, Andy and Gerry aboard with me. It was a special night and we started hitting cod, good cod in the high teens. Then Andy fought it out with a cod that weighed just over 30lbs, Gerry and James both had fish to 24lbs, and I added a 27lber, and two more halibut, the best about 22lbs, as well as big haddock and lots of coalfish. Over the five days fishing the boat had 15 cod over 20lbs and ten halibut. Twice as many halibut as all the other boats put together. It had been a cracking trip for everyone, and I was pleased that some basic ground work had proven worthwhile with the ten halibut being the best result possible. We didn't win the competition, the German team did. We finished fourth by just one point, but we did enjoy some fantastic fishing and learnt a lot too, which is what fishing is all about. Did we regret not going for the coalfish...no!

HALIBUT OFF THE SHORE

I'd long wanted to catch a 10lb-plus halibut off the shore. Apart from a small one in Iceland, and the Havoysund escapee, that was as close as I'd got. Halibut were not really on my mind when I went back to Norway in February of 2011 to a place called Hasvig, near Zanzibar Inn, Flatanger. I was part of a group put together by Ian Peacock, which included Gary Pye, an experienced and successful match angler from the Northeast, also Steph Monaghan from Glasgow, a work colleague. We would be shore fishing mainly. It was bitterly cold, though surprisingly the locals told us that there had been little snow that winter, and the ground was mainly clear of snow. Unusual conditions to say the least. They said it had affected the fishing, and the fishing proved not that easy. However Gary and I fished the first night with Gary getting a cod of 13lbs. Over the next few days we all had cod to 7lbs or so.

On the fourth day I had the option to fish with a couple of other lads at a quarry on the Einvika road. I chose to fish where a channel started to narrow towards an island, though this was well outside casting distance. I set up with only one rod, and chose to fish a pennel pulley rig so that if a fish was hooked the lead weight would pull upwards above the fish and reduce any chance of the lead weight snagging on any rocks. I made the rig from 80lb mono so that there was strength in the rig should I hook a big cod or maybe a wolfish. I was fishing on my own, with the other lads a good 100 yards or so away. I realised that in front of me the water dropped down in to about 20 meters, but just 25 feet out was a shallow, near vertical rock ledge that any fish I hooked would have to be lifted over.

Shore halibut rig

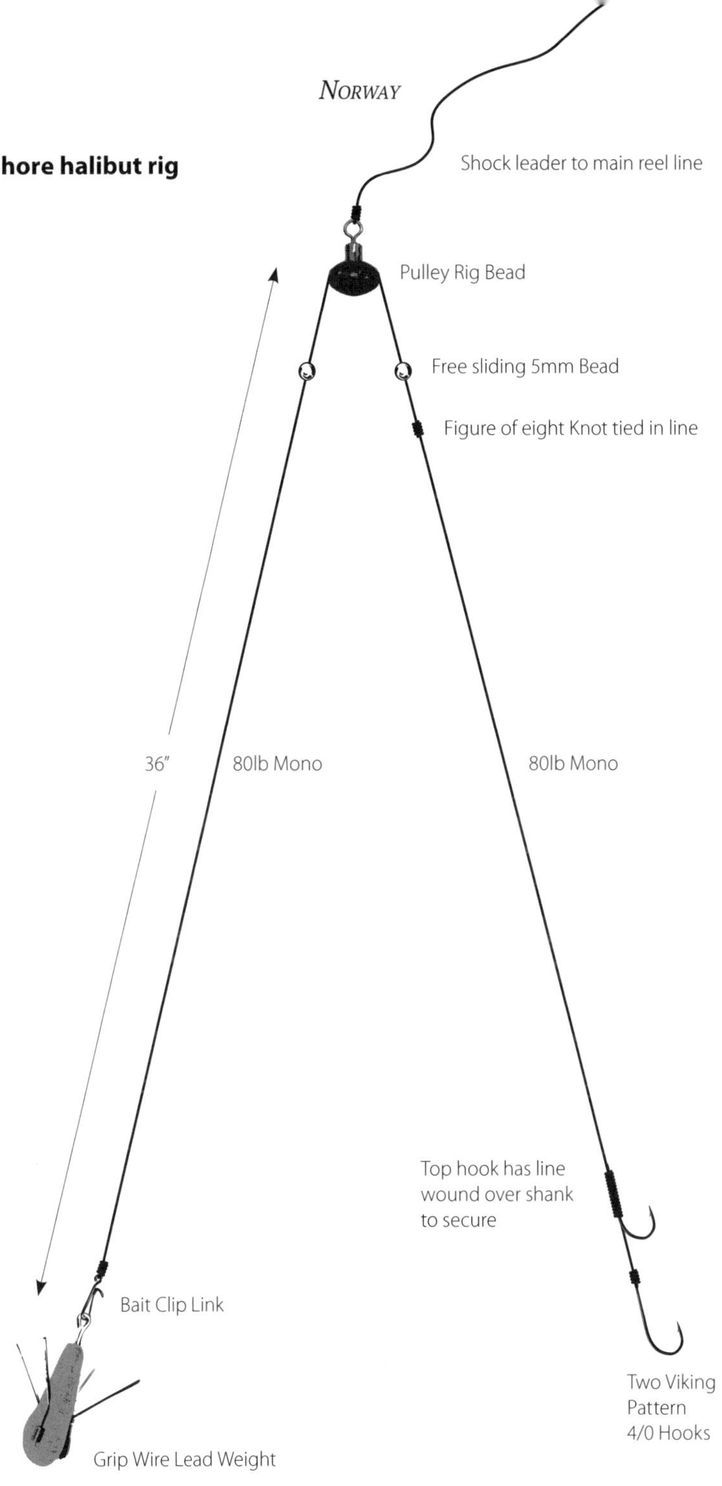

I caught small codling to 3lbs or so immediately, with some small haddock, but towards slack water I cast out a big half bluey body and decided to leave this there for as long as possible to try and pull in a bigger fish. I was thwarted first cast by a another greedy 3lb codling. I cast again and let the bait settle. Tightened the line so that the rod tip was just taking on the pressure of the line to the lead weight. Little more than 10 minutes later, I saw the rod tip dip slightly, then again. Without warning the rod tip pulled over and the butt lifted up off the ground in the rod rest as a fish made off with the bait. I instinctively grabbed the rod, wound down until I felt the weight of the fish, then struck to set the hook. Whatever I'd hooked was heavy, and very determined to put some distance between it and me.

The fish, on feeling the line pressure, powered off on an unstoppable run. I watched a good 30 meters of line disappear off the reel in that first near constant run. I could feel the fish undulating across the seabed, and I knew instantly what I'd hooked. The fish paused now, then ran again taking more line. It was about minus 12C, yet I was sweating. I was keeping heavy pressure on the fish, trying to turn it and stop the fish taking more line that might find a rock or snag out in the depths. The fish went to ground, stuck to the seabed like gum. Pressure gradually moved it, and it accelerated away again taking more line. It made several more short runs, then I was able to retrieve a good amount of line against a very heavy weight. It went to ground again out in front of me. I used this to my advantage and put maximum rod pressure on the fish. Grudgingly it moved, and when it did, I kept it coming. I could not see the fish but forced it towards and then over the rock ledge in front of me in one pull. The fish, as it cleared the ledge, suddenly came in to view. It was a halibut and it looked big. It now started to swim parallel back and forth in front of me. The fish turned its head and tried one last time to gain its freedom, but it lacked the strength. I let it swim in front of me some more to fully tire it out. I'd shouted for the other lads and one of the guys arrived and showed no hesitation in going in to the water to lift the fish out. It was a thick, solid set fish, and we weighed it at 15lbs 10ozs. I had my double figure shore halibut. Not the biggest halibut, but still a fish I will always remember as it was one I'd targeted for some time.

Halibut are an infectious species. They fight way above their muscular weight using every ounce of their energy against you. The dive for the seabed, even from a 20lb fish, is breath taking. Off the shore a sizeable fish will run far and hug the seabed putting maximum pressure on you. They are a special fish. Anglers are often asked, if they could fish for only one species, what would it be? For me, the halibut would be a real contender.

Reluctantly we now leave the snow kissed land of Norway and its magical fish with just one last glance at those magical mountains bathed in the midnight sun. Time for one last cast maybe?

Chapter 15
No Such Thing As One Last Cast

I have to admit, that initially, the thought of writing this book was a little daunting. I wanted to do it. I first wrote books in the late 1980s, so it was not new to me. What changed was that the feature writing became the mainstay of my work, and the thought of new books had to be forgotten. After more than a 25-year gap it was a big step to begin again. Once the first paragraph of the first chapter was written, I knew I'd made the right decision to write this book. It may be selfish, but I realised it was a means by which I could relive all the highs and lows, feel the tension and anxiety during the playing of the big fish, and take in again the sights and sounds of the magical places I've been. Also to remember special people and the conversations we exchanged. It was a look back at pretty much my whole life and that addiction to angling.

There is a misconception amongst anglers that those who write in the magazines have the opportunity to fish every day. It is not so. Like everyone, the necessity to earn a living is ever present, and that means being productive. As a professional angling journalist now for well over 30 years, my working life was spent initially in front of a loud and clicky typewriter. The keys heavy and laborious to pound. Now I work on a sophisticated MacBook Pro laptop. Writing, like fishing, is a continual learning curve, and the advance of technology, you would think, would contribute to freeing up time. Again, it is not so. I find I work the same or more hours, but I'm much more productive in real terms. In reality I try to fish at least once, hopefully twice, a week.

Sometimes, due to work commitments, it may be as long as three or four weeks inbetween wetting a line. It has been as long as six weeks. If I cannot fish for such a long period, I find myself day-dreaming of the surf, the rocks, the roll of the boat, the clean, fresh, ocean air, and the cry of the gulls. Though I am a writer, and comfortable that I made the appropriate choice of career, it is still not truly me, just a part of me. I am an angler, first and foremost.

Before beginning to pen these pages. I went back to the very place, that wondrous door to my future, where I caught that first flounder and where I spent so much of my early fishing years. It has changed, but not too much. The estuary channel is different, its silted up some, and is less wide than I remember. The mud banks that form the little crab filled bays seem higher too. Walking across the slate coloured rocks to where it narrows to a near point and enters the mystical waters, I see the little flat rock that I first fished from. It seems smaller than I remember, but it is there, just as it was, ignorant of time, tide and man. Sat on the rock it feels so familiar. The rhythmical lap of the waves, the sway of the weed at my feet, the breeze in the trees behind, and the swirl of a fish as it works up the channel. They are all there as if no time has passed at all. Though time has passed, sat contemplating on the rock, I realise the boy is still in me. I am the same as I was at the outset of this life journey. Fascinated by what lies beneath the deep, dark water.

Back in late March, this book nowhere near finished and a mountain of normal work in front of me, and having not fished for over three weeks, I desperately needed my fishing fix. I went to North Wales with Clive Griffiths. The fishing was subdued and hard. We were targeting the seasons first plaice, but bites were scarce. I caught a couple of small dabs and whiting, then, just after low water, I saw the belly in the deliberate slack line I'd left between the rod and the lead weight lift and drop back. I knew it was a plaice. I waited for the belly in the line to lift again. When it did, I picked up the rod and wound in to the fish. I was right, it was a plaice. It was still thin and recovering from the rigours of spawning. It weighed 1lb 8ozs and will be over 2lbs when its enjoyed a full summers feeding. To me the first plaice is the harbinger of spring, a sign that winter has let go her icy fingers in the sea and on the land. From here on in, the fishing just gets better and better.

Though the book has been a pleasure to write, my work is nearly done. It is now time to fish. It is June, 2015. The bass are feeding hard on the rough ground beaches and I yearn to feel the rod tense and pull hard over in my hands as a fish sucks in a big crab bait. The tope are running thick and fast inside Cardigan Bay. The trout are taking the nymph and rising to the dry fly, and there's a chance of a sea trout or salmon in the river. The offshore wrecks are loaded with fat prime pollack, and the huss and wrasse are feeding off the rock ledges. It is time... time to fish!

Many many books about fishing in the past have titled their last chapter 'One Last Cast'. The last editorial page of magazines over the years have often followed suit. One last cast! What a terrible final thought! When I finish fishing at the end of the day or night, there is never a thought of one last cast. The cast that ends that day is the cast before my next cast when I fish again somewhere new. I am addicted to angling. It is my life. For me there is no such thing as one last cast!

Acknowledgements

During the course of an angling lifetime, a huge number of people have made a major contribution to my fishing via help, advice and above all, just by being good company. Here are a few I owe a major debt too.

In the early days the writers encompassed within the bible that was *Angling Magazine*. Ian Gillespie, Digger Herrington, the editor Brian Harris, and most of all John Darling. Their features and knowledge opened up a new world to me, a world I would live in for the rest of my life.

Bob Hawkes, the editor of the original *Sea Fishing Magazine* back in the late 1980s, is a man I will never forget. Bob was a Hot Metal Press man. He could spot a spelling mistake or grammatical error at 20 paces. He saw something in me no other did. His encouragement for me to write, and his early guidance, proved a major turning point in my life. For that I am eternally grateful!

Rob Wyatt, a product developer I worked with for many years. We started as work colleagues, but became, and remain, real friends, a friendship that has now spanned almost a quarter of a century. Someone who, when I need a solid, sensible, grounded opinion, that's exactly what I get. Norman Dunlop was a professional Sea Angling Advisor for the Fisheries Board in Ireland. We worked together for over 20 years, and still fish together today. I've learnt a lot about fishing when alongside Norm, but also benefitted greatly simply by his good company. Mike Patton, a Fisheries Officer from Donegal, is another long time colleague, fishing friend, and someone always bursting with enthusiasm and a pleasure to work and fish with. Mike Hennessy, again a Fisheries Officer from Kerry in Ireland. We've worked together for a long time now, and Mike's contribution to my collection of species, and success in getting magazine features when up against tight deadlines and difficult conditions, has been huge. Colin Albert, originally from Aberystwyth but now Cardiff based, a friend and when possible fishing companion for close on 30 years, someone who has always been there to help and bounce ideas off.

I've deliberately left my fishing buddy, Clive Griffiths and my son Mike Jr to last. No angler could have had a better mate to fish with than Clive. Some of the fish in this book would never have been landed without his enthusiasm, and sometimes sheer bravery in taking on the elements to land a big fish for me. What's more, rain, shine, catch or blank, we have a laugh, and that is also what fishing should be all about.

Mike Jr, without a direct push or nudge from me, is also an angler in the true sense of the word, but more so my friend, confidante, fishing buddy and, when it comes to modern technology, my guru. A better son a man could not have! To all of the above, and to so many others, thank you!

Mike Thrussell

Abu Garcia
LEEDA
Abu Garcia
PENN